C16 Machine Language for the Absolute Beginner

First Published in the United Kingdom by Melbourne House

This Remastered Edition
Published in 2021 by
Acorn Books
www.acornbooks.co.uk

This book is a page-by-page reproduction of the original 1985 edition as published by Melbourne House. The entirety of the book (apart from a final publisher feedback section) is presented with no changes, corrections nor updates to the original text, images and layout; therefore no guarantee is offered as to the accuracy of the information within.

Contents

FOREWORD

So. you've had your C16 for a while and you've been using BASIC to write programs to do simple tasks. You've slowly been exploring and experimenting with your new computer.

Maybe you've used your computer to run some professionally written software: word processing, accounting systems, educational software or games.

You may have wondered what it is that makes these programs so different to the ones you have been writing in BASIC. These professional programs seem to be able to do many tasks at the same time, including functions which you may have not realised that your computer can do.

Apart from the size of the programs, and the amount of time spent in writing them, the one major difference between your programs and most of the programs that you will buy in a store, is that most professional programs are written wholly or partly in machine language.

Machine language is a must for the really serious programmer. Most games, useful utilities and interface programs are written in machine language.

This book attempts to give you an introduction to the world of machine language, the other side of your Commodore 16.

You will be led through the microprocessor's instruction set slowly at first, practising each instruction learned using the monitor/program.

As we work through the instruction set you will meet new concepts and features of your computer, some of which you may not have known it possessed.

You are encouraged throughout the book to check that the computer's output is what you would logically expect it to be. Keep a pen and paper close at hand to copy on paper what the microprocessor is doing to get its answers and to see if your answers agree.

Appendices with explanations are supplied at the back of the book and you will often be referred to these in the text of the book. The rest are provided to give you some information to continue on after you have finished working your way through this book. A list of commonly used terms is also provided if you become confused by the terms used in the book.

Chapter 1
Introduction to Machine Language

One advantage of machine language (M.L.) is that it allows the programmer to perform several functions to which BASIC is not suited. The most remarkable advantage of machine language, however, is its speed. On the C16 you can carry out approximately 100,000 M.L. instructions per second. BASIC commands are several hundred times slower.

This is due to the fact that BASIC is written in machine language and one single BASIC command may be a machine language program of hundreds of instructions. This is reflected in the capabilities of each of the languages.

Machine language instructions, as you will see as you work your way through this book, are extremely limited in what they can do. They perform only minute tasks and it takes many of them to achieve any 'useful' function. They perform tasks related to the actual machinery of the computer. They tell the computer to remember some numbers and forget others, to see if a key on the keyboard is pressed, to read and write data to cassette tape, and to print a character on the screen.

Machine language programs can be thought of as subroutines — like a subroutine in BASIC — a program within another program that can be used anywhere in the program and returns to where it was called from when it is finished. You use the commands GOSUB and RETURN to execute and then return from a subroutine.

.
.
.
.

10 GOSUB 1000

.
.
.
.

10000 RETURN

.

2

This wouldn't be a very useful subroutine because it doesn't do anything but it does show how a subroutine works.

Using a machine language program

To call a machine language subroutine from a BASIC program you use the command "Sys address". Just as with the GOSUB command you must tell the computer where your subroutine starts. "GOSUB 1000" calls the subroutine at line number 1000. Similarly "Sys 1000" calls the machine language subroutine at memory address 1000.

NOTE here that memory address 1000 is very different to line number 1000. A memory address is not a program line number, it is the 'address' of an actual piece of memory in the computer.

Memory addressing

You have heard that the C16 has 16K of memory. 16K represents the number of individual pieces of memory in the computer. Each piece of memory can be thought of as a box which can contain one character, one piece of information.

With over 16,000 separate boxes the computer must have a filing system to keep track of them, so that it can find each separate piece of information when it needs it. The filing system it uses gives each box an 'address', which is like the address of your house. You use addresses to find the one particular house you are looking for anywhere within a busy city. You use this address to visit a house, to send it mail or to pick up a parcel from it. The computer, like us, sends information and moves from one place (subroutine) to another using its system of addresses.

The computer's system of addressing is simpler than ours — for it anyway — as it starts at one end of memory and calls it address zero. It then counts through the memory 'boxes', giving each of them a number as it goes — from zero at one end to 65535 right at the other end of the memory. For us this would be very difficult to remember but for the computer it is the logical way to do things. These numbered boxes can be thought of as post office boxes. If you put something in the box at address number one, it will stay there until you put something else in there in its place.

Each box can hold only one thing at a time. When you put something else in a box, what was originally there will be lost forever.

The command "Sys 1000" tells BASIC to execute a machine language subroutine whose first instruction is stored in the box at address 1000.

Using memory directly from BASIC

There are two other basic commands you will find extremely useful in this work.

They enable us to put things in and collect things from the boxes in memory. These commands are "PEEK" and "POKE". Print PEEK (5000) picks up the contents of the box at memory address 500 and prints it. This can be used like any other function within a BASIC program, e.g. Let A = PEEK (387) or LET C = 7*PEEK (1078) + 14.

POKE 1100,27 puts the number after the comma, in this case 27, into the box at memory address 1100, e.g. POKE 2179,B or POKE C,X. Try this:

PRINT PEEK (5000)
POKE 5000, 200
PRINT PEEK (5000)

We will be using these BASIC commands a lot while experimenting with machine language instructions so that we can find out the results of the programs we write and use. BASIC will be a tool by which we will write, run, and observe our machine language programs.

Machine language as a subroutine

You have read our machine language programs will be used like a subroutine in BASIC. In place of the "GOSUB" we use the "SYS" command.

In BASIC, as you know, a subroutine must end with the command RETURN.

.
.
.
.

GOSUB 1000

.
.
.
.

1000 ....

....

1020 RETURN

So too our machine language routines must end with a command to RETURN to the main program but it will not be a BASIC command, it will be a machine language instruction.

The machine language instruction for RETURN is ---- 96 ----. That's it, just 96. 96 is what the microprocessor understands as a command to RETURN from a subroutine. It would of course be impossible for us to remember that 96 is RETURN as well as a list of hundreds of other instructions, so we have names for each instruction. These names are

4

meaningless to the computer but, hopefully, make some sense to us, the programmers. These names are short, simple and to the point and are called Mnemonics.

The mnemonic for 96 is RTS. RTS stands for RETURN from Subroutine. Where necessary throughout we will provide both the machine code numbers and the mnemonics of an instruction, as this makes it readable to you while at the same time providing the information the computer needs.

To demonstrate how this works we will create a very **short** machine language program. Type in the following BASIC line:

POKE 8192,96

This puts 96 (the value of the RTS instruction) into the box at memory address at location 8192.

Congratulations, you have just created your first machine language program. It doesn't do much; it is just like the empty BASIC subroutine

GOSUB 400

400 RETURN

Sitting in the box at memory address 8192 is the instruction 96 (RTS).

We will now run it just to check that it works using the command "Sys". Type in the following BASIC line:

SYS 8192

The computer should respond with READY. It has just executed your program.

Chapter 1 SUMMARY

1. Assembly code is fast. It allows access to computer inbuilt hardware functions that are not convenient to use from BASIC.

2. Commands have very minor functions which they can perform.

3. Memory is "addressed" using numbers from 0 to 65535.

4. A memory address can be thought of as a post office box, which can only hold one piece of information at a time.

5. PEEK is used to examine the contents of a memory location from BASIC.

6. POKE is used to put something into a memory location from BASIC.

7. Sys is used to run a machine language program from BASIC.

8. The value 96 (RTS) must be placed at the end of every machine language program to tell the computer to "RETURN from subroutine".

Chapter 2
Basics of Machine Language Programming

Using memory from machine language

So far we have discussed MEMORY, discussed how you can look at things in memory from BASIC, and how to put things in memory from BASIC.

This of course has to be done within our machine language programs as well. We need to be able to pick up some information from one of the boxes in memory, perform operations on it and then return it to the same, or to a different, box in memory. To do this the microprocessor has devices called registers. These can be thought of as hands which the microprocessor uses to get things done.

The registers

There are three of these hands (registers) called A, X and Y, each of which is suited to a particular range of tasks in the same way that a right handed person uses his right hand to play tennis, his left hand to throw the ball in the air to serve, and when needed both hands, e.g. to tie his shoes.

These hands (registers) can pick up information from the memory boxes. Like memory they can only hold one piece of information at a time, but they are not themselves a part of the memory as they have no address. They are an actual part of the microprocessor and there are special machine language instructions which deal with each of them separately.

The accumulator

The first register we will talk about is the 'A' register (or Accumulator). As you will see in the following chapters, the accumulator's functions are the most general of the computer's hands. It is also the register which handles most of the microprocessor's mathematical functions.

In most cases the microprocessor must be holding some information in one of its hands (registers) before it can do anything with it. To get the microprocessor to pick up something from one of the boxes in memory, using the accumulator, you use the instruction "LDA". This mnemonic stands for load accumulator. This loads the contents of one of the boxes in memory into the microprocessor's accumulator hand, e.g.

LDA 253

This command takes the contents of the box at memory address 253 and puts it in the microprocessor's A hand (accumulator). The machine code value of this command is 165 253.

NOTE here that the machine code is in two parts. Unlike the command RTS which is in one part, −96−, the LDA 253 has one part for the command LDA,−165−, and one part for the address of the box in memory which contains the information being picked up, −253−. These two parts of the instruction are put in separate memory boxes so the boxes containing the program | LDA 38 | would look like: | RTS |

| 165 |
| 38 |
| 96 |

Addressing modes

Most machine language instructions have several different forms or modes, which allow the programmer flexibility in choosing how and where he will put his data in memory for his program to operate on. There are eight different forms for LDA alone, called Addressing Modes.

In various different ways, these addressing modes alter the way in which the address of the box in memory to be used is specified within the instruction.

For example, assume you had an instruction to take a letter out of a certain post office box. Your instructions could tell you to do this in several different ways:

1. You could be told to look for box number 17.

2. You could be told to look for the box third from the right on the second bottom row.

3. You could be told to look for the box owned by Mr. Smith.

4. You could be told to look for the box whose address was contained in a different box.

5. You could simply be handed the letter.

You will find out more about addressing modes later in the book, but for now you will be introduced to three of the eight different forms of the LDA command.

Mode 1 — 165 253   LDA 253

This is a short form of the LDA. For reasons which will be explained later, it can only access memory over a small range of possible addresses. This short form is called zero page addressing.

Mode 2 — 173 55 4   LDA 1079

This is a longer form of the LDA command; it can access a box anywhere in memory. NOTE here that the machine code is in three parts. The first part — 173 — is the command for LDA in this three part form. The — 55 — and the — 4 — represent the address of the box 1079 which contains the data to be put in the A hand. The reasons for this apparently strange number which makes 1079 into 55,4 will become clear in the following chapter. This mode is called absolute addressing.

Mode 3 — 169 71   LDA # 71

This command is different from the previous two. Instead of looking for the information to be put in the accumulator in one of the boxes in memory, the information you want is given to you as part of the instruction. In this case the number 71 will be put in the accumulator. It has nothing at all to do with the box at address number 71. This is like example number on page 8. Note here that this different type of addressing known as 'immediate' addressing is shown in the mnemonic by a '#' symbol before the number.

We now know how to get the microprocessor to pick something up from memory, but before we can do anything useful we have to know how to get the microprocessor to do something with it. To get the microprocessor to place the contents of its A hand (accumulator) in memory, we use the instruction STA which stands for Store Accumulator. This puts the contents of the accumulator in a specified box in memory.

This instruction too has several addressing modes (seven in fact) but only two of them will be discussed here.

Mode 1 — 133 41   STA 41

This instruction puts the contents of the accumulator in the box at address 41. As in the LDA, the similar instruction in two parts (zero page mode) can only reach a limited number of addresses in memory boxes.

Mode 2 — 141 57 03   STA 825

This is like Mode 1 except that it can put the contents of the accumulator in a box anywhere in memory (absolute addressing). The – 141 – specifies the instruction and the – 57 – and the – 3 – contain the address of box 825 (this is explained in Chapter 3).

QUESTION: Why is there no 'STA' immediate mode (see LDA # 71)?
ANSWER: The 'immediate' mode in 'LDA # 71' puts the number in the instruction – 71 – into the accumulator, somewhat like being handed a letter, not just a post office box number of where to find the letter. STA immediate mode would attempt to put the contents of the accumulator in the STA instruction itself. This is like being told to put a letter not into a post office box but into the instructions you have been given. Obviously this has no practical meaning.

Simple program input routine

We will now write a few machine language programs to examine the instructions we have learned so far. To make it easier, enter the following basic program:

```
5      PRINT CHR$ (147); "......"
10     REM THIS PROGRAM WILL MAKE IT EASIER TO ENTER
       MACHINE CODE PROGRAMS
20     READ A
30     IF A = –1 THEN GOTO 70
40     POKE 8192 + X, A
50     X = X + 1
60     GOTO 20
70     PRINT "BEFORE . . . –LOCATION 3072 "; PEEK (3072)
80     SYS 8192
90     PRINT "AFTER . . . –LOCATION 3072 "; PEEK (3072)
100    END
1000   DATA 169, 1 : REM LDA#1
1010   DATA 141, 0, 12 : REM STA 3072
1020   DATA 96 : REM RTS
9999   DATA – 1
```

LINES 1000-9999 contain our machine language program.
LINES 20-60 puts our program from data statements into memory boxes starting from 8192 so it can be run.
LINES 70-90 print "BEFORE" and "AFTER" tests on the memory we are getting our machine language program to change.

When the basic program is finished, our machine language program will be contained in memory boxes as follows:

Address	Data
8192	169
8193	1
8194	141
8195	Ø
8196	12
8197	96

For the programmer's benefit this is written out in mnemonic form as follows:

8192	LDA #1
8194	STA 3Ø72
8197	RTS

Assembly language

A program written out in mnemonic form is called an 'assembly languge' program, because to transform this list of letters which can be understood by the programmer into a list of letters which can be understood by the microprocessor, you use a program called an 'assembler'. Throughout the book we will give you programs in both formats:

address	code			mnemonics
8192	169	1		LDA#1
8194	141	Ø	12	STA 3Ø72
8197	96			RTS

Our basic program, as well as placing our machine code in memory, runs our program (see line 8Ø).

You will see by our before and after analysis of memory address 3Ø72 that it has been changed by our program as we intended. The original value of location 3Ø72 could have been anything. The number you see **may** change each time you run the program. It is impossible to know what will be in memory **before** you put something in there yourself, just as you can't tell what might be left over in a post office box you haven't looked into before. The value in memory address 3Ø72 after the program has been run is :1. This shows that our program did what was expected — it loaded the number 1 into the accumulator and then stored it into memory at 3Ø72.

Screen memory

There is one result from this program which you may not have expected. Look at the top left hand corner of the screen. You will see it contains an 'A'. Line 5 of the program clears the screen, and nowhere in the basic program was the 'A' printed on the screen, therefore it must have been put there by the machine language program. We know the machine language program puts the value 1 into location 3072. Could this print an 'A' on the screen? Try it from BASIC and see what happens. Press the CLR to clear the screen. Type:

POKE 3072,1

You will see that the 'A' has reappeared on the top left corner of the screen. This has happened because memory at 3072 has a dual purpose. It is used to display things on the screen, as well as carrying out the remembering functions at normal memory. The post office box description is still valid, but now the boxes seem to have glass fronts so that you can see on your screen what the boxes have inside them. If you look at the table of screen display codes in appendix 14, you will see that for the value 1 that we placed in location 3072, the character that should be displayed is an 'A'. (SET 1 is used by default. To change the character set being used, press the commodore key and the shift key at the same time.)

Let's try to display some of the other characters in the table on the screen. Let's try to print an 'X' on the screen. First we need to look up the table of screen display codes to find the value corresponding to the letter 'X'. You will find that this value is 24. To put this in memory at address 1024 we will use the program we wrote earlier:

LDA # 1
STA 3072
RTS

But this time we will change the LDA # 1 to a LDA # 24. Using the same BASIC program to put this into memory, we must first change line 1000 which holds the data for the LDA command. This must now read:

1000 DATA 169,24   :REM LDA # 24

Our machine language program will now (when the basic progam is run) read:

8192	169	24		LDA # 24
8194	141	0	12	STA 3072
8197	96	0		RTS

When this is run you will now see an 'X' appear in the top left hand corner of your screen.

At this stage you might ask, how do I print something somewhere else on the screen? The answer is simple. 'Screen Memory' (these 'glassfronted' boxes) exists in memory from 3072 all the way through to 4071. It is set up in 25 rows of 40 columns as you see on your screen. Memory at 3072 appears on the top left corner, 3073 appears next to that to the right, and 3074 next to that. Similarly 3072 + 40 (3112) appears immediately under 1024 on the left edge at the second top row and 3112 + 40 (3152) under that, and so on.

Using the same basic routine to enter our program, we will now try to print on the row second from the top of the screen. The address of this place on the screen is given by 3072 + 40 (screen base + 1 row) = 3112.

Therefore we want our program to be:

LDA # 24   Character 'X'
STA 3112   First column Second row
RTS

To do this we change the data for our program on line 1010 to read:

1010 DATA 141, 40, 12   :REM STA 3112

The machine language program will now print an 'X' on the second line from the top of the screen.

Printing a message

We will now use our BASIC program to write a bigger program which will write a message on the screen. Type the following lines:

1000   DATA   169,8
1010   DATA   141,0,2
1020   DATA   169,5
1030   DATA   141,1,2
1040   DATA   169,12
1050   DATA   141,2,2
1060   DATA   141,3,2
1070   DATA   169,15
1080   DATA   141,4,2
1090   DATA   96

Now run the program. You will see that it has printed "HELLO" at the top of the screen. The machine language program we wrote to do this was:

Address	MACHINE CODE			ASSEMBLY CODE	
49152	169	8		LDA # 8	SCREEN DISPLAY CODE FOR 'H'
49154	141	0	4	STA 3072	
49157	169	5		LDA # 5	SCREEN DISPLAY CODE FOR 'E'
49159	141	1	4	STA 3073	
49162	169	12		LDA # 12	SCREEN DISPLAY CODE FOR 'L'
49164	141	2	4	STA 3074	
49167	141	3	4	STA 3075	
49170	169	15		LDA # 15	SCREEN DISPLAY CODE FOR 'O'
49172	141	4	4	STA 3076	
49175	96			RTS	

Check the values used with those given in the table of screen display codes.

It is interesting to note the way in which the two 'L's were printed. There was no need to put the value 12 back into the accumulator after it had been stored in memory once. When you take something from memory, or when you put something from one of the registers (hands) into memory, a copy is taken **and** the original remains where it started.

We can write the same programs we have just written using different addressing modes. It is useful to be able to write the same program in different ways for reasons of program efficiency. Sometimes you want a program to be as fast as possible, sometimes as short as possible, and at other times you will want it to be understandable and easily debugged.

We will change the program this time to give us greater flexibility in what we print. Type in the following lines:

```
15      INPUT "LETTER VALUE"; B : POKE 3, B
1000    DATA 165, 252              : REM LDA 3
1090    DATA 169, 23               : REM  LDA # 23
1100    DATA 141, 5, 12            : REM STA 3077
1110    DATA 96                    : REM  RTS
```

Our machine language program will now look like this:

Address	MACHINE CODE			ASSEMBLY CODE
49152	165	252		LDA 3
49154	141	0	4	STA 3072
49157	169	5		LDA # 5
49159	141	1	4	STA 3073
49162	169	12		LDA # 12
49164	141	2	4	STA 3074
49167	141	3	4	STA 3075
49170	169	15		LDA # 15
49172	141	4	4	STA 1028
49175	169	23		STA 3076
49177	141	5	4	LDA # 23
49180	96			STA 3077

NOTE that this finds the value at its first letter from the box at memory address 3 using zero page addressing instead of immediate addressing. Line 15 of our basic program sets this box in memory to be any number we choose. Run this program several times choosing the values 25, 2 and 13.

We have seen in this chapter how memory can have more than one function by the example of the memory between 3072 and 4071, which doubles as screen memory. Similarly other parts of memory can have

13

special functions. Different areas of memory are used to control screen colours, graphics, sprites, sound, the keyboard, games controllers (joystick) and many other I/O (input/output) functions. These areas will be referred to throughout the book on a purely introductory level. We encourage you to find more detailed descriptions from more advanced texts, e.g. 'Commodore 16 Exposed', C. Duffy and R. Woolcock, published by Melbourne House.

Chapter 2 SUMMARY

1. The microprocessor uses registers (like hands) to move things about and to work on memory.

2. It has three general purpose hands (A(accumulator), X and Y).

3. We use the LDA command to get the microprocessor to pick something up in the accumulator (A hand).

4. We use the STA command to get the microprocessor to put the contents of the accumulator into memory.

5. These commands and many others have several different addressing modes which allow us flexibility in the way we store and use our data:
   • immediate addressing holds the data within the instruction,
   • absolute addressing uses data stored anywhere in memory,
   • zero page addressing uses data stored within a limited area of memory.

6. A program written out in mnemonic form is called an assembly code program.

7. Memory is used to display information on the screen.

8. Information is displayed according to a screen display code which gives a numeric value to any printable character.

9. Memory is used to control other I/O (input/output) functions of the computer.

Chapter 3
Introduction to Hexadecimal

Uses of hexadecimal

So far in this book we have talked about memory in several different ways, but we have not been specific about what it can and cannot hold. We have used memory to hold numbers which represented characters, numeric values, machine code instructions and memory addresses. We have merely had to put a number we want in memory without thinking how the computer actually stores it, in all but one case. It is the absolute addressing mode which has shown us that the computer's numbering system is not as simple as we might have at first thought, e.g. 141 5 12 is the machine code for STA 3077. The 141 represents the STA, leaving the numbers 5 and 12 signifying the address 3077. There is obviously something going on here which we have not accounted for.

We have previously compared the microprocessor's registers and memory to hands. How big a number can you hold in your hand? Well that depends on what we mean by hold. You can use your fingers to count to five, so you can use one hand to hold a number from zero to five. Does that mean the biggest number you can hold is five? You may be surprised to know that the answer is NO.

Counting from 0 to 5 on your fingers like this

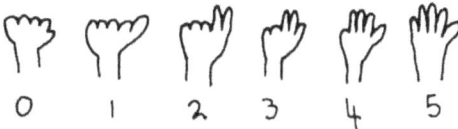

is very wasteful of the 'resources' of your hand, just as counting like that on a computer would be wasteful of its resources.

Binary

A computer's 'fingers' can either be up or down (on or off) but, as with your fingers, it can tell which of its 'fingers' is on and which is off. In other words, the value represented depends not only on the number of fingers used but on the position of those fingers. Try this yourself. Give each finger one of the following values (write it on in pen if you like).

Now try to count by adding the numbers represented by each finger in the up (on) position:

Try to represent the following numbers on your fingers: 7, 16, 10, 21, 29.

Q. What is the biggest number you can represent on your fingers?
A. $1+2+4+8+16 = 31$

As you can see 31 is quite a significant improvement on our original effort of 5. The computer's 'hands' are different from ours in several ways. Its fingers are electronic signals which can either be on or off, as opposed to our fingers being up or down. For the programmer's benefit the condition on is given the value 1 and the condition off is given the value 0. The other major difference is that the computer has eight 'fingers' on each 'hand'. This may sound silly, but there is no reason for it not to be that way. As it turns out it is a fairly easy setup to handle. The computer's eight fingered hand is called a 'byte' of memory. As with our own fingers, we give each of the computer's 'fingers' one of the following values: 1, 2, 4, 8, 16, 32, 64, 128.

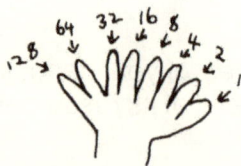

Again we count by adding together the values of all those fingers in the 'on' position.

16

Eight fingered hand	Computer's 'hand' — byte	Number
	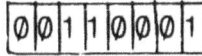	32+16+1 = 49
	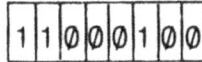	128+64+4 = 196
	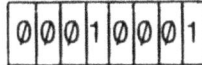	16+1 = 17

Q. What is the biggest number that can be represented by the computer's 'eight fingered hand'?

A. 128+64+32+16+8+4+2+1 = 255

Without realising it, what we have done in this chapter is introduce the binary numbering system (base two). All computers work in base 2 representing electrical on's and off's by an endless stream of 1's and 0's. This of course would make the programmer's task of understanding what is going on inside the computer even more confusing than it already is, e.g.,

Assembly Code	MACHINE CODE	BINARY
LDA #8	169 8	10101001 00001000
STA 3077	149 5 12	10010101 00000101 00001100
RTS	96	01100000

Why hexadecimal?

This of course would be impossible for a programmer to remember, and difficult to type correctly. We could of course just use decimal as listed in the machine code column. As it turns out, this is not the most convenient form to use. What we do use is hexadecimal or base sixteen. This may sound strange but it becomes very easy to use because it relates closely to the actual binary representation stored by the computer.

To convert between binary and hexadecimal is easy. Each hexadecimal digit can store a number between 0 and 15 just as each decimal digit must be between 0 and 9. Therefore one hexadecimal digit represents one half of a byte (eight fingered hand).

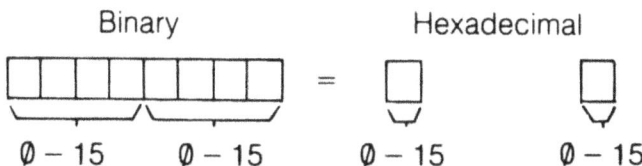

The whole eight fingered hand can be shown by two hexadecimal digits. You might be wondering how one digit can show a number between one and fifteen. Well it is exactly the same as decimal but the numbers 10, 11, 12, 13, 14 and 15 are represented by the letters A, B, C, D, E, F respectively.

BINARY	DECIMAL	HEXADECIMAL
0000	0	0
0001	1	1
0010	2	2
0011	3	3
0100	4	4
0101	5	5
0110	6	6
0111	7	7
1000	8	8
1001	9	9
1010	10	A
1011	11	B
1100	12	C
1101	13	D
1110	14	E
1111	15	F
10000	16	10

This shows that converting from binary to hexadecimal is merely dividing into easy-to-see segments of four (fingers).

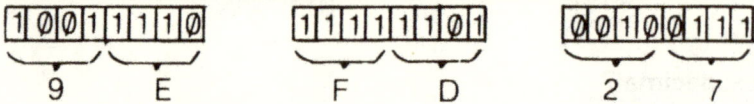

1 0 0 1	1 1 1 0		1 1 1 1	1 1 0 1		0 0 1 0	0 1 1 1
9	E		F	D		2	7

Hex and binary mathematically

Mathematically any base 10, 2, 16 or 179 follows a simple format. Each digit takes the value Ax (BASE) Position-1

In other words in decimal 98617 is

$$7 \times 10^0 + 1 \times 10^1 + 6 \times 10^2 + 8 \times 10^3 + 9 \times 10^4 \quad = 98617$$
$$7 \times 1 + 1 \times 10 + 6 \times 100 + 8 \times 1000 + 9 \times 10000 = 98617$$
$$7 + 10 + 600 + 8000 + 90000 \qquad\qquad = 98617$$

In binary 01011101 is

$$1 \times 2^0 + 0 \times 2^1 + 1 \times 2^2 + 1 \times 2^3 + 1 \times 2^4 + 0 \times 2^5 + 1 \times 2^6 + 0 \times 2^7 = 93$$
$$1 \times 1 + 0 \times 2 + 1 \times 4 + 1 \times 8 + 1 \times 16 + 0 \times 32 + 1 \times 64 + 0 \times 128 = 93$$
$$1 + 0 + 4 + 8 + 16 + 0 + 64 + 0 \qquad\qquad = 93$$

In hexadecimal A7C4E is

$14 \times 16^0 + 4 \times 16^1 + 12 \times 16^2 + 7 \times 16^3 + 10 \times 16^4$ = 687182
$14 \times 1 + 4 \times 16 + 12 \times 256 + 7 \times 4096 + 10 \times 65536$ = 687182
$14 + 64 + 3072 + 28672 + 655360$ = 687182

Several points should be noted here. Firstly, any number which can be stored in one memory box (a number from 0 to 255) can be stored in 8 binary digits (bits), or as we have been calling them till now 'fingers'. Any number from 0 to 255 can also fit in two hexadecimal digits (FF = 15 x 16^1 + 15 x 1 = 255). This, however, is where our problem with absolute addressing occurs. If we can't put a number bigger than 255 into memory, how do we specify an address which may be between 0 and 65535 (64K)? The solution is to use two boxes, not added together but as part of the same number. When dealing with addresses we are dealing with 16 finger (16 bit) (2 byte) binary numbers. This is the same as saying four digit hexadecimal numbers. The largest number we can hold in a four digit hexadecimal number is

$FFFF = 15 \times 1 + 15 \times 16 + 15 \times 256 + 15 \times 4096$
$= 15 + 240 + 3840 + 61440$
$= 65535 = \textbf{64K}$

which is large enough to address all of memory, e.g., the 2 byte (16 byte) hex number 13A9 equals

1	3	A	9
0001	0011	1010	1001

$13 \times 16^2 + A9 \times 16^0$
$13 \times 256 + A9$
$= 4864$

For example, the 2 byte hex number 0405

$= 4 \times 256 + 5$
$= 1024 + 5$
$= 1029$

Absolute addressing

If you look back to the beginning of this chapter you will see that this is the problem associated with absolute addressing which we have been trying to solve. One other thing to remember with absolute addressing is that the bytes of the address are **always** stored backwards, e.g.,

LDA   1029
= 141   5   4

The most significant byte (high byte) − 4 is placed last, and the least significant byte (low byte) − 5 is stored first. NOTE this is opposite to normal, e.g., normally 17 where 1 is the most significant digit (1 × 1∅) and is stored first. The 7 (7 × 1) is least significant and comes second. For some reason the bytes of an absolute address are always stored low byte, high byte.

This chapter also explains zero page addressing. Two byte instructions leave only 1 byte to specify the address, e.g., LDA 38 − 165 38. We have said before that when using 1 byte we can only count from ∅ to 255. Therefore zero page addressing can only address the first 256 bytes of memory. A block of 256 bytes is called a page.

To specify the fact that we are using hexadecimal this book follows the standard practice of placing a $ sign before a hexadecimal number.

LDA 3∅72   is the same as LDA $∅C∅∅
LDA 65535   is the same as LDA $FFFF
LDA ∅   is the same as LDA $∅

From now on all machine code listings will also be shown in hexadecimal,

Address	MACHINE CODE $			ASSEMBLY CODE	
49152	A9	8		LDA	#$8
49154	8D	∅	12	STA	$∅C∅∅
49157	A9	53		LDA	#$53
49159	8D	1	12	STA	$∅C∅1
49162	6∅			RTS	

irrespective of the format used in the assembly code, which will vary depending on the application.

Converting hexadecimal to decimal

We have provided in appendix 3 a table for quick hexadecimal to decimal conversions. To use this chart for single byte numbers, look up the vertical columns for the first hexadecimal (hex) digit and the horizonal rows for the second digit, e.g.,

$2A − 3rd row down
      11th column from left
Printed there is   LO   HI
                  | 42   1∅752 |

Look at the number under LO (Low byte). 42 is decimal for $2A hex. For 2 byte hex numbers divide into 2 single bytes. For the left byte (or high byte) look up under HI and add to the low byte LO, e.g.,

$7156   divide HI = $71   LO = $56
HI − 71 − 8th row down
          2nd column from left

LO	HI
113	28928

LO – 56 – 6th row down

7th column from left

LO	HI
86	22016

Add high and low 28928 + 86 = 29014

$7156 = 29014

NOTE: in all cases

LO	HI
X	Y

$Y = 256 * X$

The high byte is 256 times the value of the same low byte.

Chapter 3 SUMMARY

1. In counting on a computer's 'fingers', position (which fingers), as well as the number of fingers, is important.
2. Each of the computer's hands and each piece of memory has 8 'fingers', and the biggest number they can hold in each is 255. ,
3. An eight 'fingered' piece of memory is called a byte.
4. Each finger has a value which depends on its position. Value = Position -1   1, 2, 4, 8, 16, 32, 64, 128 Binary.
5. Hexadecimal (base sixteen) is the grouping together of binary. 1 Hex digit = 4 binary digits. Hex is easier to handle than binary or decimal.
6. DECIMAL 0 1 2 3 4 5 6 7 8 9 10 11 12 13 14 15 16 17 18
   HEX   0 1 2 3 4 5 6 7 8 9 A B C D E F 10 11 12 etc.
7. Zero page addressing can access the first 256 bits, the maximum addressable by 1 byte.
8. Absolute addressing can access 65536 (64K) bytes of memory (all), which is the maximum addressable by 2 bytes.
9. Absolute addresses are **always** stored low byte first then high byte, e.g. 8D 98 17 LDA $1798.
10. Hexadecimal numbers are specified by prefacing them with a $ sign.
11. Remember the quick conversion table for hex to decimal in Appendix 3.

Chapter 4
Introduction to Tedmon

Tedmon is a built-in machine language monitor (M.L.M.), mini assembler, and disassembler, that remains resident as part of the C16's ROM chip. It is used as an aid in the entry and debugging of machine language programs, and is also useful as a tool for examining any area of memory that the user so desires.

Like BASIC, Tedmon has a series of commands that require strict adherence to a set of syntactical rules. Be sure that when using Tedmon, you use the formats exactly as they are shown below. The commands supported by Tedmon are as follows:

A   Assemble a line of 6502/7501 machine code. This command makes the entry of standard 6502/6510 mnemonics very simple. Being merely a one line assembler, it does not support such fancy 'extras' as macros or labels. Use the following format to assemble a line of source code:

.A (address) (mnemonic) (operand)

For example:

.A 1000 LDA #$08

You should find that as soon as you press the <RETURN> key, your line of source code will be expanded to include the hexadecimal values of the mnemonic and any additional parameter/s that may have been specified. The above example would be expanded to give:

.A 1000 A9 08 LDA #$08

Once a line of source code has been successfully assembled, the monitor will display the next legal address for assembly, on the following line. If you do not wish to continue assembling, you should simply press <RETURN> to exit from this mode. If the monitor detects an error in the format of the line for assembly, it will display a question mark (?), at the end of the line.

C Compare one area of memory with another area, and report on the differences. The compare command is used in the following manner:

.C (start address) (end address) (with address)

Example:

.C 2000 2FFF 3000

This command will compare the contents of memory locations $2000 to $2FFF with the contents of memory locations $3000 to $3FFF, and will display any memory of those that do not hold equivalent values with the ones they are being compared with. For example, if the following memory locations held the following values:

$0100 - $02 $0200 - $02
$0101 - $03 $0201 - $02

and the command:

.C 0100 0101 0201

then the number '0101' would be displayed, signifying that the location with which it was compared (i.e. $0201), contained a different value.

D Disassemble an area of memory. The 'D' command can be used to disassemble any area of memory that is required. It takes the following format:

.D (start address) (optional end address)

Here are examples of the two legal formats for this command:

.D 1000

or alternatively

.D 1000 3000

The first example will display a disassembly of 10 lines of object code. The second example will disassemble any object code found between memory locations $1000 and $3000. A special note should be taken at this stage, with regard to the use of the 'D' command. You may find that upon disassembly of a given area of memory, that the disassembler gives output that is garbage. An example might be:

```
.     1000    02           ???
.     1001ˉ   AF           ???
.     1002    20 02 AF     JSR $AF02
.     1005    02           ???
etc
```

23

You will notice that the first two lines are not intelligible, but that the third line shows a proper instruction, followed by another line of garbage. In this case it must be pointed out that due to the lack of constraints regarding memory usage when writing in machine code, areas of memory can be used for any purpose. In the above example, we would be wise to assume that the memory from $1000 to $1005 holds data or something of the like, but due to the fact that the disassembler has rejected so many bytes, it does not seem like part of a machine language program.

F   Fill an area of memory with the specified byte/s. This command can be used to fill up an area of memory with any hexadecimal value ($00-$FF). It takes the following form:

.F (start address) (end address) (value)

Example:

.F 1000 4000 00 will fill the area of memory from $1000 to $4000 with the value of zero.

G   Begin execution of a machine language program, as specified by the memory address, or the current contents of the stored program counter. This command is used to 'run' a machine language program, from within the monitor. It takes the form:

.G (address)

For example:

.G 2FE0

or simply

.G

The first example will jump to the machine language program starting at memory location $2FE0. The second example will jump to the location, as specified by the value of the stored value of the program counter (see the 'Register' command). Care should be taken that there is in fact a machine language program at the location specified. Jumping to a location that contains garbage could lead to a situation whereby the only means to recover use of your machine would be to turn it off and then on again.

H   Hunt through memory, for a specific byte or series of bytes, reporting any occurences. The hunt command is one of the most useful commands that Tedmon supports. It is used to search through a given area of memory for a single byte or series of bytes, as specified for the command:

.H (start address) (end address) (data) (. . .)

24

Example:

.H 1000 2000 08

would display the locations (if any), between $1000 and $2000, that contain the value of 8.

.H 1F00 3000 01 06 03

will display the location (if any) which contains the value of 1, only if the following two bytes contain the values 6 and 3 respectively. This command is extrememly handy when trying to locate a particular sequence of data, or even a series of instructions. For example, we want to locate any occurences of the following machine code sequence between locations $2000 and $3000:

. A9 05 LDA #$05
. 85 01 STA $01

Now the method for finding this sequence is as simple as:

.H 2000 3000 A9 05 85 01

The 'Hunt' command can also be used to find a string of characters, in ASCII representation, by placing the string of characters after an apostrophe:

.H 30E0 4000 'HELLO'

will search the area of memory from $30E0 to $4000 for the word 'HELLO'

Load a program or data, from the tape or disk drive. This command acts in much the same way as the basic 'LOAD' command. The only major difference is that this command ALWAYS loads a program into the area of memory that it was previously saved from i.e. it acts like:

LOAD"FILENAME",8,1

or:

LOAD"FILENAME",1,1

in the case of tape users.

The syntax for the 'L' command is as follows:

.L"FILENAME",(device)

A couple of examples might be:

.L"CAT",08

for disk, or:

.L"DOG",01

for tape users.

M Examine an area of memory, as specified by a start and end address. This command is used to examine an area of memory for its contents. You will find that this command will probably be the most frequently used, alongside the 'Disassemblē' command:

.M (start address) (end address)

For example:

.M 1000

or:

.M 1000 2000

The first example will display twelve lines of data signifying the contents of the memory locations starting with location $1000. The second example will display the contents of memory locations $1000 to $2000. An example of the output from the 'Memory' command is given below:

.M 1000 1008
. 1000 01 02 03 04 05 06 07 08 . . . .
. 1008 41 42 43 44 45 46 47 48 ABCDEFGH

You will notice that the memory locations are displayed in rows of 8 hexadecimal numbers. To the right of these numbers you will see their equivalent ASCII representations (reversed). If it so happens that the monitor program is unable to convert the contents of a memory location into a displayable ASCII equivalent, (e.g. 0, because CHR$(0) is invisible), then it simply places a reversed full stop in that position.

R Examine the contents of the 6502/7501 Registers. This command is used to examine the current contents of the stored values of the 7501's various registers. Its syntax is as follows:

.R

This will give the display:

	PC	SR	AC	XR	YR	SP
;	0000	00	00	00	00	F8

where:

PC = The current value of the program counter.
SR = The current value of the status register.
AC = The stored value of the 7501 accumulator.
XR = The stored value of the 'X' register.
YR = The stored value of the 'Y' register.
SP = The stored value of the stack pointer.

It should be pointed out that these values are not the actual values that are in the various registers; after all, the monitor itself is a large machine language program, and is changing the values of these registers constantly. These values are actually stored in memory, and are loaded from there into the registers upon the execution of a 'G'oto command. Before entering a machine language program, these registers may be changed at will (see the ';' command).

S   Save a file or data, to the tape or disk. The 'Save' command is like the BASIC save command, in that it allows the user to save a program to tape or disk. You will find that the monitor's Save command is far more flexible, in that it allows you to specify the start and the end address of the block of memory that you wish to save. The 'S'ave command takes the following format:

.S"FILENAME", (device), (start address), (end address)

Some examples might be:

.S"PROG",01,0C00,0A00

for tape, or:

.S"HELLO",08,0C00,0A00

for a save to disk.

T   Transfer the contents of an area of memory, to another location. The transfer command is very useful for copying away areas of data, or setting up a duplicate of a program in memory. It is used in the following way:

.T (start address) (end address) (new start location)

An example of a transfer could be:

.T 1000 1FFF 3000

The above example will copy the area of memory from $1000 to $1FFF to the area from $3000 to $3FFF.

V   Verify that a program on tape or disk, is the same as that in memory. This command acts in the same way as the BASIC 'verify' command. It will compare a program on tape or disk, with the area of memory that it was saved from, reporting on any differences with an error return. This becomes a handy aid in determining whether a program was saved to tape or disk without error:

.V"FILENAME", (device)

You might use:

.V"BLOQD",01

for tape users, or:

.V"BONES",08

for disk users.

X eXit from Tedmon, back into BASIC. Typing:

.X

will simply return the user from the monitor, back into BASIC.

. Assemble a line of 6502/7501 machine code (same as A) (see the 'A'ssemble command).

> modify memory locations, as specified by a memory address (see the 'M'emory command).

; modify the 6502/7501 registers. This command allows the 7501 stored registers to be updated prior to the use of the 'G'oto command.

To enter Tedmon, simply type:

MONITOR

You should now be greeted with the display:

```
     PC    SR   AC   XR   YR   SP
;   0000   00   00   00   00   F8
```

which denotes the 6502/7501 registers and their contents. Underneath this display you should see the familiar flashing cursor — the sign that Tedmon is awaiting a command.

At this stage, you are free to use any of the above commands. You should also note that you will not have any access to the wide range of 'BASIC' commands while you are in the monitor. To re-enable these commands, you will have to use the 'X' command, which will return you to BASIC.

It is suggested that you familiarize yourself with Tedmon by trying a few of the above examples, as well as a few of your own. This will enable you to gain confidence in the somewhat contrasting environment of extremely strict syntax, which prevails within Tedmon. It should soon become clear that the Tedmon monitor will be an invaluable tool in the devolopment of machine language programs for your C16.

Chapter 5
Microprocessor Equipment

In the previous four chapters we have covered a lot of the groundwork needed to understand the intricacies of machine code programming. More of the basics will be introduced as we go on. We have covered enough at this stage to move on to such things as using machine language to do some arithmetic.

Storing numbers

We know from Chapter 3 that the largest number we can store in a single byte (memory location) is 255. We have also seen that for addresses bigger than 255 we could use two bytes to represent them in low byte/high byte format so that Address = low byte + 256 × high byte.

Surely then we could use the same method to represent any sort of number greater than 255 and less than 65536 (65535 = 255 + 256 × 255), and in fact if necessary this can be taken even further to represent even higher numbers:

Numb = 1st byte + 256 × 2nd byte + 65536 × 3rd byte + . . . etc.

The carry flag

Now, when we add two 1 byte numbers together it is possible that the result is going to be bigger than 255. What then can we do with the result of the addition? If we put the result in one byte it could be no bigger than 255, so

$$207 + 194 = 401 \bmod 255 = 145$$

but also

$$58 + 87 = 145$$

Surely there is something wrong here. We must somehow be able to store the extra information lost when a result is larger than 255. There is provision for this within the 7501 microprocessor in the form of a single

29

bit (single finger) 'flag' called the carry flag. The carry flag is 'set' (turned on) if a result is greater than 255, e.g.,

$2\emptyset7 + 194 = 145$; carry $= 1$
$58 + 87 = 145$; carry $= \emptyset$

NOTE: a single bit **is** large enough to cover all possible cases of carry.

```
  11111111        255
+ 11111111       +255
 ⌐1 1111111∅      254 + carry
 carry bit
```

Therefore to add two 2 byte numbers together, you add the low bytes first, store the result, and then add the high bytes including the carry bit from the addition of the low bytes, e.g.,

$3\emptyset A7 + 2CC4 = 5D6B$

is done in the following manner:

low bytes
```
  A7
+ C4
  6B      carry = 1
```
high bytes
```
  3∅
+ 2C
+  1      (carry bit)
  5D
```
Answer $= 5D6B$

Adding numbers

To handle this, the machine language instruction to add two 1 byte numbers together is ADC (add with carry). This adds the specified number (or memory) to the accumulator and leaves the result in the accumulator. The instruction automatically adds in the carry bit to its calculation. Therefore since the carry bit could be set to anything before you put something in it yourself (like memory — see Chapter 1), it is necessary to set the carry to zero before an addition if that addition does not want to add the carry of a previous calculation. To set the carry flag to zero we use the instruction CLC (Clear Carry flag) before such ADC's.

Type in the following program using the monitor (Tedmon):

```
2000  LDA #$00
2002  STA $05
2004  LDA #$03
2006  CLC
2007  ADC #$05
2009  STA $05
2008  BRK
RUN
```

From within the monitor type .G 2000. Now type .M 0005. Location $05 should contain the value of 08.

We will now change the program to alter the sum we are performing. Type:

```
2000  LDA #$00
2002  STA $05
2004  LDA #$27
2006  CLC
2007  ADC #$F4
2009  STA $05
2008  BRK
```

Then type .G 2000, to execute the program.

Type .M 0005. The value stored in $05 will be $1B. Since $F4 + $27 is actually $11B, and thus the carry flag would have been set.

NOTE: we cannot tell the carry has been set from our results.

We will now change the program again. This time we will deliberately set the carry using the SEC (Set Carry Flag) command before doing our addition. Type the following lines:

```
$2000  LDA #$03
$2002  SEC
$2003  ADC #$05
$2005  STA $05
$2007  BRK
```

Enter and execute the program, using .G 2000. Now type .M 0005. You will notice that location $05 contains the value $09, i.e. our program has added:

```
      3
  +   5
  +   1   (carry)
  _____
  =   9
```

From these examples we see how the carry bit is 'carried' along from the result of one addition to another.

We will now use this to do an addition of two 2 byte numbers using the method we have described previously.

Two byte addition

Suppose we want to add the numbers 6C67 and 49B2.

```
  6C67
+ 49B2
= ????
```

To do this we must separate the problem into two 1 byte additions:

```
low bytes   67       high bytes   6C
          + B2                  + 49
          1 19                  + 1 (carry)
           carry                 B6
```

Type the following:

```
2000  LDA #$67
2002  CLC
2003  ADC #$B2
2005  STA $03
2007  LDA #$6C
2009  ADC #$49
200B  STA $04
200D  BRK
```

This will store the low byte of the result in $03 and the high byte of the result in $04.

ENTER and RUN the program using .G 2000.

Type .M 003 and join the high byte and low byte of the results to give the answer:

```
  6C67
+ 49B2
  B619
```

Subtracting numbers

This procedure can be extended to add numbers of any length of bytes.

The microprocessor, as well as having an add command, has a subtract command. Similar to the ADC command the SBC (Subtract with Carry) uses the carry flag in its calculations. Because of the way in which the microprocessor does the subtraction, the carry bit is inverted (1 becomes 0 and 0 becomes 1) in the calculation, therefore

```
      8                    8
    - 5      but         - 5
    - 1                - CARRY   (CARRY = 1)
  = ___                = _____
      2                    3
```

Consequently, to do a subtraction without carry, the carry flag must be set to 1 before the SBC command is used. Type the following:

```
2000  LDA #$08
2002  CLC
2003  SBC #$05
2005  STA $05
2007  BRK
```

ENTER and then RUN this program, using .G 2000.
Use .M 0005 to examine the result.

You will see by the results that clearing the carry instead of setting it has given us the wrong answer. We will correct our mistake by setting the carry to 1 before the subtract. Change the 'CLC' at $2002 to 'SEC' and re-run it, using .G 2000.

Examine location $05, using .M 0005

You will now see that we have the correct answer.

```
      8                      8
    - 5                    - 5
    - 1 (CARRY=0)         - 0 (CARRY=1)
  = ___                  = ___
      2                      3
```

You may have wondered how the microprocessor handles subtractions where the result is less than zero. Try for example 8 − E = −6. Change the line 'SBC #$05' to 'SBC #$0E' and rerun the program.

```
      8      or        BORROW = 108 carry cleared to zero
    - E                    - E
    - 6                    ___
                            FA
```

NOTE: that − 6 = 0 − 6 = FA
FA + 6 = 0

This clearing of the carry to signify a borrow can be used for multibyte subtraction in the same way as it can for multibyte addition. Try to write a program to do the following subtraction:

E615 − 7198

Here is an example:

```
2000 LDA #$15
2002 SEC
2003 SBC #$98
2005 STA $03
2007 LDA #$E6
2009 SBC #$71
200B STA $04
200D BRK
```

ENTER and RUN this, noting the results. Combine the high and low bytes of the result to get the answer 747D, from memory locations $03 and $04.

These instructions ADC and SBC can be used in many addressing modes, like most other instructions. In this chapter we have only used immediate addressing.

NOTE: SEC and CLC have only one addressing mode — implied. They perform a specific task on a specific register, so there are no alternatives to its addressing. Their method of addressing is 'implied' within the instruction.

An exercise

Write a program to add the value $37 to the contents of memory location $05 using ADC in the 'absolute' addressing mode, and put the result back there. Use .M 0005, to observe the results.

NOTE here:

```
LDA #$FF
CLC
ADC #$01
```

leaves the value $0 in A with the carry set, and

```
LDA #$00
SEC
SBC #$01
```

leaves the value $FF in A with the carry clear (borrow).

Therefore we have what is called 'wraparound'. Counting up past 255 will start again from 0, and downwards past zero will continue from 255 down.

Chapter 5 SUMMARY

1. Any size number may be represented by using more than 1 byte.
   Numb = 1st byte + 2nd byte × 256 + 3rd byte × 65536 + . . . etc.

2. The 75Ø1 microprocessor has a carry flag which is set to signify the carry of data into the high byte of a two byte addition.

3. ADC adds two bytes plus the contents of the carry flag. A CLC should be used if the carry is irrelevant to the addition.

4. ADC sets the carry flag if the result is greater than 255, and clears it if it is not. The answer left in the accumulator is always less than 256. (A = Result Mod 256)

5. SBC subtracts memory from the accumulator and then subtracts the inverse of the carry flag. So as not to have the carry interfere with the calculations, an SEC should be used before the SBC.

6. SBC sets the carry flag if the result does not require a borrow (A − M $\geq$ Ø). The carry is cleared if (A − M < Ø) and the result left in A is 256 − (A−M).

7. Two byte addition:
```
        CLEAR CARRY
XX = ADD LOW BYTES + (CARRY = Ø)
YY = ADD HIGH BYTES + (CARRY = ?)
Result = $YYXX
```

8. Two byte subtraction:
```
        SET CARRY
XX = SUBTRACT LOW BYTES − INVERSE (CARRY = 1)
YY = SUBTRACT HIGH BYTES − INVERSE (CARRY = ?)
Result = $YYXX
```

Chapter 6
Program Control

Looping using JMP

There is an instruction for this — it is the JMP (JUMP) instruction. Like BASIC's 'GOTO' you have to tell the 'JMP' where to jump to in the form JMP address (JMP Low Byte High Byte) (ABSOLUTE ADDRESSING).

We will use this command to create a program equivalent to the following BASIC program.

INITIALISE

.

100 X=X+4
110 GOTO 100

.
.

In order to give you some idea of what is actually happening while the program is executing, we will add the value of 4 to screen memory, at $0C00. Type the following program in, using Tedmon:

```
.2000 LDA #$00
.2002 STA $0C00
.2005 LDA $0C00
.2008 CLC
.2009 ADC #$04
.200B STA $0C00
.200E JMP $2005
```

Then type .G 2000 to start the program executing. You should notice that there is a flickering square in the top left corner of your screen. Characters are being displayed very quickly within this square.

Infinite loops

You will also notice that the program is still going. Just like the program

```
100 X = X + 4
110 GOTO 100
```

our program will go forever around the loop we have created. This is called being stuck in an 'infinite loop'.

The RUN/STOP key will not get us out of the loop. There is a machine code program which is part of BASIC which tests to see if the runstop key is being pressed, but our program does not look at that keyboard. There are only two ways of getting out of a machine code infinite loop. One way is to press RUN/STOP and RESET keys at the same time. This will stop the computer and return it to BASIC. The other way to stop the program is to turn the computer off. Press RUN/STOP RESET to stop the program. You will now be in BASIC. To continue with our program intact type:

MONITOR, to return you to Tedmon.

There is no other way to exit a machine language routine unless it returns by itself using an RTS. NOTE that because of the JMP, the program is never able to exit, as in the following BASIC program:

```
5  X = 4
10 PRINT "HELLO";X
15 X = X + 4
20 GOTO 10
30 END
```

Obviously the END statement is never reached here either because of the GOTO at line 20.

To get this program to print HELLO 4 to HELLO 100 we would write:

```
5  X = 4
10 PRINT "HELLO";X
15 X = X + 4
20 IF X = 104 GOTO 40
30 GOTO 10
40 END
```

Here line 20 will GOTO line 40 only if X = 104 and the program will go through to the END statement and stop. If X is not equal to 104, the program will go through to line 30 and continue around the loop to line 10. To do this in machine language we need one instruction to compare two numbers (X and 104) and another instruction to JUMP depending on the result of the comparison (IF . . . GOTO 40).

Comparing numbers

We have previously (see Chapter 5) met the idea of a flag. It is a single bit (single finger) value held inside the microprocessor. In Chapter 5 we met the carry flag which was set to signify the need for a carry in a multibyte addition (or borrow in multibyte subtraction). The microprocessor has seven flags for different purposes which it keeps in a special purpose register called the Processor Status Code Register (or Status Byte). These seven flags (and one blank) are each represented by their own bit (finger) within this byte and have special microprocessor commands dealing with them. These flags are set or reset by most machine code commands. (More will be said about them in Chapter 10.) For example, ADC sets or resets the carry flag depending on the result of the addition. Similarly 'CMP' (Compare), which compares the contents of the accumulator with the contents of a memory location (depending on addressing mode), signifies its results by setting or resetting flags in the status byte.

Branch instructions

The other instruction we said we would need to write our program, is one which would jump to an address dependant on the values of the processor status flags. This form of instruction is called a 'branch' instruction. It is different to the JMP instruction not only in the fact that it is conditional (dependent on the conditions of the status flags), but it is unique in that it uses the relative addressing mode. Relative addressing means that the address used is calculated relative to the branch instruction. More will be said about relative addressing and the way branch instructions work at the end of this chapter.

Zero flag

To test if the result of a CMP instruction is that the two numbers compared were equal, and branch if they were, we use the BEQ (Branch on Equal) command.

Try the following program, which differs from our last one in that the program will stop if the value of memory location $0C00, is equal to $80.

.2000 LDA #$00	.200C CLC
.2002 STA $0C00	.200D ADC #$04
.2005 LDA $0C00	.200F STA $0C00
.2008 CMP #$80	.2012 JMP $2005
.200A BEQ $2015	.2015 BRK

We have managed to find a way to use a loop that tests for a condition on which to jump out of the loop. We could however make this more efficient by creating a program that looped until a certain condition is reached. The difference is subtle but it is shown by this BASIC program in comparison to the previous one.

```
 5 X = 4
10 PRINT "HELLO";X
15 X = X + 4
20 IF X <> 104 GOTO 10
30 END
```

To accomplish this short program, line 20 would require the use of the 'BNE' (Branch if not equal to), if we were to convert this to machine language. Type:

```
2000 #$04
2002 STA $0C00
2005 LDA $0C00
2008 CLC
2009 ADC #$04
200B STA $0C00
200E LDA $0C00
2011 CMP #$80
2013 BNE $2005
2015 BRK
```

As you can see, there are many ways to write a program. Which is right and which is wrong no one can say but the better program is, on the whole, the one which is most readable and easiest to debug. This is the most efficient way to write the most efficient code.

There is a lot we can learn by knowing how an instruction works. The CMP instruction for example compares two numbers by doing a subtraction (accumulator − memory) without storing the result. Only the status flags are set or reset. The instructions we have just used (BEQ and BNE) do not refer their 'equalness' to the numbers being compared. They in fact test the status registers 'zero' flag, and stand for:

BEQ − Branch on Equal to Zero

BNE − Branch on Not Equal to Zero.

It is the condition of the zero flag which is set by the result of the subtraction done by the CMP command (accumulator − memory = 0 which sets the zero flag = 1). This flag is then tested by the BEQ or BNE command. This may seem to be a meaningless point until you realise that, since the CMP command is done by a subtraction, the carry flag will also be set by the result. In other words if the subtraction performed by the CMP needs a 'borrow' (A − Mem < 0, A less than memory), then the carry will be cleared (CARRY = 0). If the subtraction does not need a 'borrow' (A − Mem $\geqslant$ 0, A greater than or equal to memory), then the carry will be set (CARRY = 1).

Therefore the CMP command tests not only A = Mem but also A <
Mem and A≥Mem and therefore (if A≥Mem but A ≠ Mem) then A >
Mem. We can now write our BASIC program:

```
 5  X = 4
10  PRINT "HELLO";X
15  X = X + 4
20  IF X < 101 GOTO 10
30  END
```

This makes the program a little more self explanatory. It shows clearly
that values of X bigger than the cutoff 100 will not be printed. To test for
the accumulator less than memory, you use CMP followed by BCC
(Branch on Carry Clear) because a borrow will have occurred. To test for
the accumulator greater than or equal to memory, use CMP followed by
BCS (Branch on Carry Set).

Relative addressing

All branch instructions use an addressing mode called relative
addressing (JMP is **not** a branch instruction.) In relative addressing the
address (the destination of the branch) is calculated relative to the
branch instruction. All branch instructions are two bytes long — one
byte specifying the instruction and the other specifying the address in
some way. This works by the second byte specifying an offset to the
address of the first byte **after** the instruction according to the tables in
Appendix 4. From 0 − 7F means an equivalent branch forward and from
80 − FF means a Branch backward of 256 − the value. Therefore:

```
        F0 03              BEQ tohere
        8D 34 03           STA $334
tohere  60                 RTS
```

will be the same no matter where it is placed in memory.

The value 3 as part of the branch isntruction is the number of bytes
from the beginning of the next instruction (8D).

```
1st next byte (34)
2nd next byte (03)
3rd next byte (60)
```

With the following programs, check that the destination address of the
branch is in fact the address of the instruction after the branch plus the
offset value, e.g.,

```
2000  BEQ $2004
2002  STA $05
2004  BRK
```

and

```
3000  BEQ $3004
3002  STA $05
3004  BRK
```

The machine code remains the same but the disassembled version differs. The program will work exactly the same at either address. This is completely opposite to the case of the JMP which uses absolute addressing and cannot be 'relocated' (moved to another memory address).

Chapter 6 SUMMARY

1. The command JMP address is equivalent to BASIC's GOTO linenumber command. It makes the program 'Jump' to the address specified.

2. To break out of an 'infinite loop', press RUN STOP/RESET.

3. The microprocessor's STATUS CODE Register has seven flags (and one blank) which are set by many machine code instructions.

4. Branch instructions jump conditional on the state of the flag referred to by the instruction, e.g.

BEQ Branch on Equal	$Z = 1$
BNE Branch on Not Equal	$Z = 0$
BCS Branch on Carry Set	$C = 1$
BCC Branch on Carry Clear	$C = 0$

5. The CMP instruction compares two bytes (by doing a subtraction without storing the result). Only the flags are set by the outcome.

Flags	CARRY	ZERO	Signifies
	0	0	$A <$ Mem
Value	?	1	$A =$ Mem
	1	?	$A \geqslant$ Mem
	1	0	$A >$ Mem

6. Relative addressing mode, used only for branch instructions, specifies an address relative to the instruction which uses it, e.g. BNE 03 means branch 3 memory addresses forward (see table Appendix 4).

41

Chapter 7
Counting, Looping and Pointing

Counting to control a loop

Suppose we want to multiply two numbers together. There is no single machine language instruction which can do this, so we would have to write a program to do it. We could, for example, add one number to a Total as many times as the other number is Large. e.g.,

```
10  A = 7 : B = 3
20  T = T + A
30  T = T + A
40  T = T + A
50  PRINT "7*3=";T
```

It would be much easier and more practical (especially for large numbers) to do this in a loop. e.g.,

```
10  A = 7 : B = 3
20  T = T + A
30  B = B - 1
40  IF B <> 0 GOTO 20
50  PRINT "7*3=";T
```

NOTE: this is by no means the best way to multiply two numbers, but we are only interested in the instructions here. A preferred method is described in Chapter 10.

Counting using the accumulator

In this short program, unlike any other program we have dealt with previously, there are two variables. A, which we are adding to the total, and B, which controls the loop. In this case we couldn't stop our loop as we have done in the past by testing the total, because we would have to know the answer before we could write the program. Our machine language program would look, along the lines of what we have done previously, like this:

42

```
        LDA #$00
        STA A
        LDA #$03
        STA B
loop  LDA A
        CLC
        ADC #$07
        STA A
        LDA B
        SEC
        SBC #$01
        STA B
        BNE loop
        BRK
```

Counting using memory

Most of this program consists of loading and storing between the accumulator and memory. Since we so often seem to be adding or subtracting the number one from a value as a counter, or for other reasons, there are special commands to do this for us. INC (Increment Memory) adds 1 to the contents of the address specified and puts the result back in memory at the same address. The same goes for DEC (Decrement Memory), except that it **subtracts** 1 from memory.

NOTE: INC and DEC **do not** set the carry flag — they **do** set the zero flag.

Type:

```
2000  LDA #$03
2002  STA $04
2004  LDA #$00
2006  CLC
2007  ADC #$07
2009  DEC $04
200B  BNE $2006
200D  STA $05
200F  BRK
```

Program summary

$2000-2004 Initialise
$2006-200B Loop until result of DEC = 0
$200D-200F End

Using INC or DEC we can use any memory as a counter, leaving the accumulator free to do other things.

43

An exercise

Rewrite the previous program using INC and CMP to test for the end of the loop.

The X and Y registers

There are however even easier ways of creating counters than using INC and DEC. Looking back to Chapter 2, we mentioned that the 6510 microprocessor had three general purpose registers — A, X and Y. Then for the last few chapters we have been talking solely of the most general purpose register, the A register — the accumulator. So, you may now ask, what are the other 'hands' of the microprocessor, the X and Y registers, used for?

And what does 'general purpose' mean? Well, so far we have met one non-general-purpose register the processor status register (there are another two which we will meet in future chapters). The status byte can only be used to contain status flags and nothing else, as compared to the accumulator which can hold any number between 0 and 255 representing anything. The X and Y registers can, like the accumulator, hold any number between 0 and 255, but there are many functions of the accumulator that they cannot do, e.g. Add or Subtract. The X and Y registers are extremely useful as counters.

They can do the following operations (compared to those we have already discussed for the accumulator and for memory).

```
LDA  LOAD ACCUMULATOR WITH MEMORY
LDX  LOAD X WITH MEMORY
LDY  LOAD Y WITH MEMORY

STA  STORE ACCUMULATOR TO MEMORY
STX  STORE X TO MEMORY
STY  STORE Y TO MEMORY

INC  INCREMENT MEMORY ⎤
INX  INCREMENT X       ⎬ IMPLIED ADDRESSING MODE
INY  INCREMENT Y      ⎦

DEC  DECREMENT MEMORY ⎤
DEX  DECREMENT X       ⎬ IMPLIED ADDRESSING MODE
DEY  DECREMENT Y      ⎦

CMP  COMPARE ACCUMULATOR WITH MEMORY
CPX  COMPARE X WITH MEMORY
CPY  COMPARE Y WITH MEMORY
```

Using the x register as a counter

We will now rewrite our multiplication program using the X register as the counter. Type

```
LDX #$03
LDA #$00
CLC
ADC #$07
DEX
BNE L30
STA $03
BRK
```

This routine is slightly shorter and considerably faster than the original but otherwise not all that different. Rewrite all the commands using the X register, replacing them with the equivalent Y register command. Practise using the X and Y registers in place of the accumulator where possible in the programs in previous chapters.

Moving blocks of memory

How would you write a program to move a block of memory from one place to another? e.g. to move the memory from 2100 - 2150 to the memory at 2200 - 2250. Obviously we could not write it as:

```
LDA $2100
STA $2200
LDA $2101
STA $2201
    .
    .
    .
    .
    .
  etc.
```

This would be ridiculous to even attempt because of the size of the program we would have to write.

We could write the program:

```
LDA $2100
STA $2200
```

followed by some code which did a two byte increment to the address part of the instructions. This is an extremely interesting concept to think about. It is a program which changes itself as it goes. It is called 'self modifying code'. But, because it changes itself, it is very dangerous to use. It is considered very poor programming practice to use it because it is prone to errors of catastrophic proportions (writing over the wrong parts of the program and then trying to execute it will probably cause you to have to turn your computer off and on again before you can continue). Self modifying code is also extremely difficult to debug. It is an interesting concept but **do not** use it within a serious program. Self modifying code is therefore obviously not the answer to our problem.

The answer in fact, lies in addressing modes. Originally we called addressing modes ways of accessing data and memory in different ways and formats. We have so far seen:

Implied addressing

The data is specified as part of the instruction, e.g. SEC, DEY.

Relative addressing

Addressing relative to the instruction — use only in branches.

Absolute addressing

The data is specified by its two byte address in low byte, high byte format.

Zero page addressing

The data is specified by a 1 byte address and hence must be within the first 255 bytes of memory.

Indexed addressing

Our new method of addressing is called 'indexed addressing'. It finds the data to be used in the instruction by adding a one byte 'index' to the absolute address specified in the instruction. The indexing byte is taken from the X or Y register (depending on the instruction used). The X and Y registers are called 'Index' registers.

To use our post office box analogy, it is like being given two pieces of paper, one with a two byte address on it, and the other with a one byte index (∅ − 255). To find the correct box you must add the two numbers together to obtain the correct result. The number on the indexing paper may have been changed, the next time you are asked to do this.

Using the X register as an index

With this addressing mode, our program to move a block of data becomes quite simple. Type the following:

```
2000  LDX #$00
2002  LDA $24C8,X
2005  STA $24F0,X
2008  INX
2009  CPX #$28
200B  BNE $2002
200D  BRK
```

NOTE here that the mnemonic form of indexed addressing has its address field made up by the absolute address, a comma and the register used as the index, even though the following is true:

```
LDA $24C8,X
LDA $24C8,Y
```

It is the instruction, not the address field, which changes in the actual machine code. RUN the program. As you can see, we have used screen memory again to show that we have in fact duplicated a block of memory. One line on the screen will be copied onto the line below (the 6th line onto the 7th line). Be sure to have text on the 6th line to see the effect!

Non-symmetry of commands

If, as was suggested when we introduced the X and the Y registers, you have substituted the X or Y for the accumulator in some of the early programs, you may be wondering if we could do that here. The answer is no. Not all the commands can use all of the addressing modes. Neither Y nor X (obviously not X) can use the index, X addressing mode being used here with the store (STA). (It is possible to do a LDY ADDR,X but not a STY ADDR,X). For a list of all addressing modes possible for each instruction, don't forget Appendix 1.

Searching through memory

We can use the knowledge we have gained up to this point to achieve some interesting tasks quite simply. For example, if asked to find the fourth occurrence of a certain number, e.g. A9 within 255 bytes of a given address, how do we do it?

The best way is to start simply and work your way up. To find the first occurrence of A9 from F000 onwards we could write:

```
            LDY #$00
            LDA #$A9
loop        CMP $F000,Y
            BEQ found
            INY
            BNE loop
            BRK (NOT HAVING FOUND A9 from F000
            - F0FF)
found       BRK (HAVING FOUND an A9)
```

We would put a counter program around this routine:

```
            LDX #$00
COUNTLOOP   FIND 'A9'
            INX
            CPX #$04
            BNE COUNTLOOP
```

We can combine these into a single program thus:

```
            LDX #$00
            LDY #$00
            LDA #$A9
L40         CMP $F000,Y
            BEQ L90
L60         INY
            BNE L40
            STX $03
            RTS
L90         INX
            CPX #$04
            BNE L60
            STX $03
            BRK
```

In this program—when finished, if X = 4, then the fourth occurrence of
A9 was at $F000 + Y (through RTS line 120),

—if X<4, there were not four occurrences of A9 from
$F000 to $F0FF

—line 110 continues the find routine from the 'INY'. If
it started from the 'CMP' it would still be looking at
the 'A9' it found before.

ENTER and RUN this program. The results will tell you whether four
'A9's' were found. Change the program to tell you where the fourth 'A9'
was found (STY $03). ENTER and RUN it again to see the results.
Verify this using the memory DUMP command of Tedmon (.M
command).

48

Using more than one index

We will now write a program using both index registers to index different data at the same time. Our program will create a list of all the numbers lower than $38 from $F000 to $F0FF, storing them from $3000 onwards.

```
          LDX #$00
          LDY #$FF
     L30  INY
          LDA $F000,Y
          CMP #$38
          BCS L90
          STA $3000,X
          INX
     L90  CPY #$FF
          BNE L30
          STX $03
          BRK
```

X here is used as a pointer (index) to where we are storing our results. Y is used as a pointer to where we are reading our data from. NOTE here that Y starts at $FF, is incremented and so at the first $A9 the Y register contains zero.

To test for numbers less than $38 we have used CMP and BCS (A ≥ Mem see Chapter 6) to skip the store and increment storage pointer instructions. ENTER and RUN this program. Use the memory DUMP feature (.M command) to check that the numbers stored are less than $38.

Zero page indexed addressing

All the indexing instructions we have used so far have been indexed from an absolute address (absolute indexed addressing). It is also possible to index from a zero page address (see Chapter 2, zero page indexed addressing). To rewrite the previous program to look through the first 255 bytes of memory (0–255), all we need to do is change line 40 to LDA $00,Y. But, if you check with the list of instructions in Appendix 1, there is no 'LDA zero page, Y' — only 'LDA zero page, X.' We have two choices of what to do here. In practice we would probably continue using the absolute indexed instruction.

```
     BD 0000              LDA $0000,Y
```

For the purposes of this exercise, however, we will swap all the usages of the X and the Y, and use LDA zero page, X. Type:

```
LDY #$00
LDX #$FF
INX
LDA $00,X
STA $2200,Y
INY
CPX #$FF
STY $03
BRK
```

ENTER and RUN the program.

This shows that you must be careful with your choice of registers. Although they can do many of the same things, there are some commands which cannot be done by some registers in some addressing modes. It is wise to constantly refer to the list of instructions in Appendix 1 while writing programs.

Chapter 7 SUMMARY

1. INC — adds one to the contents of memory at the address specified.
2. DEC — subtracts one from the contents of memory at the address specified.
3. The zero flag (but not the carry) is set by these instructions.
4. These are used mostly as loop counters to keep the accumulator free for other things.
5. X and Y, the microprocessor's other two general purpose registers (the first being the accumulator), can be used as counters or as index registers.
6. Indexed addressing adds the value of the register specified to the absolute (or zero page) address used to calculate the final address of the data to be used.
7. Many of the instructions are similar if used on A, X or Y, but there are certain instructions and addressing modes which are not available for each register. When writing programs, make sure the instructions you are trying to use exist in the format you wish to use them in!

Chapter 8
Using Information Stored in Tables

One of the major uses of index registers is the looking up of tables. Tables may be used for many reasons — to hold data, to hold addresses of various subroutines, or perhaps to aid in complex conversions of data from one form to another.

Displaying characters as graphics

One such conversion, for which there is no formula that can be used, is the conversion from screen code to the shape of the character displayed on the screen. Normally this is done by the computer's hardware and we do not have to worry about it. When we are in graphics mode, however, this part of the computer's hardware is turned off. In normal character screen mode, our post office boxes within screen memory display through their 'glass' fronts the character which corresponds to the number stored in that box. That is, we are seeing what is in the box through some sort of 'filter' which converts each number into a different shape to display on the screen. In graphics mode, this 'filter' is taken away and what we see is each bit (finger) of each number stored throughout screen memory. For each bit in each byte which is turned on, there is a dot (pixel) on the screen. For each bit which is turned off there is a black dot on the screen.

In other words the byte $11 which looks like 0|0|0|1|0|0|0|1 would be displayed on the screen as eight dots, three black dots followed by one white dot, followed by three black dots, followed by one white dot. Depending on your television, you may be able to see the dots making up the characters on your screen. Each character is made up by a grid eight dots wide and eight dots high. Since we have just determined that we can display eight dots on the screen using one byte, it follows that to display one character eight dots wide by eight dots high, we would need to use eight bytes displayed one on top of the next.

51

For example, the character A would look like:

8 x 8 pixel grid	binary byte equivalent	hexadecimal byte equivalent

	0 1 2 3 4 5 6 7	binary	hex
0		00011000	18
1		00100100	24
2		01000010	42
3		01111110	7E
4		01000010	42
5		01000010	42
6		01000010	42
7		00000000	0

This string of eight bytes — 18, 24, 42, 7E, 42, 42, 42, 0 — is exactly what we find in the 'character generator' memory.

Graphics memory

Like the conventional text screen the high resolution graphics screen is just a section of memory. Information is put on the high res screen by writing to a particular section of memory. The graphic screen starts at 8192 and is 8000 bytes or 64000 dots in length. It's arranged as forty columns by twenty five lines of characters and each character is divided into eight rows of eight dots. Every dot can be switched on and off.

	COLUMN 0	COLUMN 1	COLUMN 2	COLUMN 39
Start of Graphics Memory	8192	8200		
	8193	8201		
	8194	8202		
	8195	8203		
ROW 0	8196	8204		
	8197	8205		
	8198	8206		
	8199	8207		
				16184
				16185
				16186
				16187
ROW 24				16188
				16189
				16190
				16191

End of Graphics Memory

Indirect indexed addressing

There will be some cases where you may be unsure as to which table you want to find your data in. In other words, imagine a program which lets you decide whether you wanted to print the message in upper or lower case letters after the program had run. You will want to use one of the two tables decided on midway through the program. This could be done by having two nearly identical programs, each accessing a different table in memory and having the beginning of the program decide which of the two to use. Of course, this is wasteful of memory. To access data by this method, there is an addressing mode called indirect indexed addressing, which allows you even greater flexibility as to where you must place your data. Indirect indexed addressing is just like absolute indexed addressing, except that the absolute address is not part of the instruction but is held in two successive zero page locations as pointed to by the indirect indexed instruction. In other words, the contents of the zero page address pointed to by the indirect indexed instruction, is the low byte of a low byte/high byte pair which contains an address which is then indexed by the index register Y to obtain the final address. (Indirect indexed addressing is always indexed using the Y register.)

Imagine the following situation, using our post office box analogy. You are handed an instruction to look in a box (zero page). The number you find in that box and the box next to it, go together to make an absolute address (low byte/high byte format). You are then told to add an index (Y) to this address to find the address you are looking for.

The mnemonic for this addressing mode is QQQ (ZP),Y
where QQQ is an instruction, e.g. LDA
    ZP   is a one byte zero page address
and the Y is outside the brackets to signify that the indirection is taken first, and the index added later. Try:

```
              LDA #$00
              STA $03
              LDA #$30
              STA $04
              LDY #$00
       LOOP   LDA ($03),Y
              STA $2600,Y
              INY
              CPY #$FF
              BNE LOOP
              BRK
```

Here a reference is made to location $3000, through the zero page locations at $03 and $04.

53

Register transfer instructions

Back in line 32 of our program, we snuck in an instruction which you hadn't previously met — TAY (Transfer A into Y). This is only one of a group of quite simple instructions used to copy the contents of one register into another.

The available instructions are:

TAX   (Transfer A into X)
TAY   (Transfer A into Y)
TXA   (Transfer X into A)
TYA   (Transfer Y into A)

These instructions are used mainly when the operations performed on a counter or index require mathematical manipulations that must be done in the accumulator and then returned to the index register.

NOTE: there is **no** instruction to transfer between X and Y. If necessary this must be done through A.

There are two addressing modes we have not yet covered which we will briefly touch on here. The first is called Indexed Indirect Addressing. No, it is not the one we have just covered, that was Indirect Indexed Addressing. The order of the words explains the order of the operations. Previously we saw indirect indexed in the form QQQ (ZP),Y, where the indirection was performed first followed by the indexing. In indexed indirect, QQQ (ZP,X), the indexing is done first to calculate the zero page address which contains the first byte of a two byte address (low byte/high byte format), which is the eventual destination of the instruction.

Imagine that you had a table of addresses in zero page. These addresses point to data or separate tables in memory. To find the first byte of these tables, you would use this instruction to index through the zero page table and use the correct address to find the data from the table you were looking for. In terms of post office boxes, we are saying here is the number of a post office box (zero page). Add to that address the value of the indexing byte (X register). From that calculated address, and from the box next to it (low byte/high byte), we create the address which we will use to find the data we want to work on.

Indirect addressing

The last addressing mode we will cover is called Indirect Addressing. There is only one instruction which uses indirect addressing and that is the JMP command.

The JMP command using absolute addressing 'Jumps' the program to the address specified in the instruction (like GOTO in BASIC).

In indirect addressing, 'JMP (Addr)', the two byte (absolute) address within the brackets is used to point to an address anywhere within memory which holds the low byte of a two byte address which is the destination of the instruction. In other words, the instruction points to an address that, with the next address in memory, specifies the destination of the jump. In post office box terms, this means that you are handed the number of a box. You look in that box and the box next to it to piece together (low byte/high byte format) the address which the JMP instruction will use. The major use of this instruction is in what is known as vectored input or output. For example, if you write a program which jumps directly to the ROM output character address to print a character, and you then want the output to be sent to the disk instead, you would have to change the JMP instruction. Using the vectored output, the program does a JMP indirect on a RAM memory location. If the disk operating system is told to take control of output, it sets up the vector locations so a JMP indirect will go to its programs. If output is directed to the screen, those memory locations will hold the address of the ROM printing routines, and your program will output through there. Here is a list of different addressing modes available on the 6510:

Implied		QQQ
Absolute		QQQ addr
Zero page		QQQ ZP
Immediate		QQQ # byte
Relative		BQQ Byte — (L # from ALPA)
Indexed	Absolute X	QQQ addr,X
	Absolute, Y	QQQ addr,Y
	Zero page,X	QQQ ZP,X
	Zero page,Y	QQQ ZP,Y
Indirect indexed		QQQ (ZP),Y
Indexed indirect		QQQ (ZP,X)
Indirect		JMP (addr)
also		
Accumulator		QQQ A

(An operation performed on the accumulator, see Chapter 10.)

Chapter 8   SUMMARY

1. In graphics mode you can 'see' the contents of screen memory. 1 bit means 1 pixel (dot on screen).

2. Characters are defined within 8 pixel by 8 pixel blocks.

3. Screen memory in graphics mode runs in character blocks, then across the screen line by line.

4. Character sets are stored in ROM.

5. Index registers are used to look up tables (among other things), using several indexed addressing modes.

6. In normal indexed addressing, the index register is added to an absolute (or zero page) address to calculate the eventual address.

7. In indirect indexed addressing, the eventual address is calculated by adding the Y register to the 2 byte address stored in the zero page locations pointed to by the 1 byte address in the instruction.

8. In indexed indirect addressing, the eventual address is calculated by adding the X register to the zero page address which forms part of the instruction. The contents of these two zero page locations specify the address.

9. The computer cannot tell the difference between meaningful and meaningless data.

10. TAX, TAY, TXA and TYA are used to transfer data between the index registers and the accumulator.

11. Indirect addressing (for JMP only) uses the contents of two bytes (next to each other), anywhere in memory, as the destination address for the jump.

Chapter 9
Processor Status Codes

We mentioned in Chapters 5 and 6 the concepts of flags within the microprocessor. We talked about the carry flag and the zero flag, and we discussed the branch instructions and other instructions associated with them, e.g. SEC, CLC, BCS, BCC, BEQ and BCC. We said that these flags, along with several others, were stored in a special purpose register within the microprocessor called the processor status code register or, simply, the status register. This register is set out, like any other register or byte in memory, in eight bits (fingers). Each bit represents a flag for a different purpose:

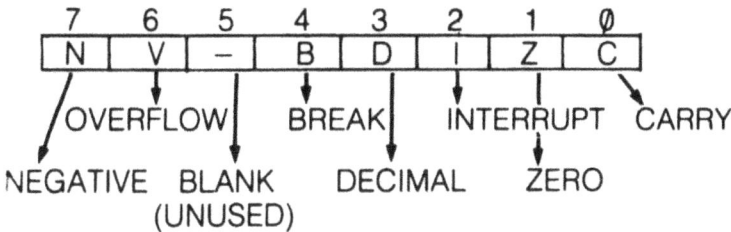

7	6	5	4	3	2	1	0
N	V	–	B	D	I	Z	C

OVERFLOW   BREAK   INTERRUPT CARRY

NEGATIVE BLANK   DECIMAL   ZERO
         (UNUSED)

A list of which instructions set which flags can be seen in the table in Appendix 1.

1. **The carry (C) flag,** as we have already seen, is set or cleared to indicate a 'carry' or 'borrow' from the eight bit of the byte into the 'ninth' bit. Since there is no ninth bit, it goes into the carry to be included in future calculations or to be ignored. The carry can be set and cleared using SEC or CLC respectively. A program can test for carry set or cleared using BCS or BCC respectively.

2. **The zero (Z) flag**, as we have already seen, is set or cleared depending on the result of an operation, comparison or transfer of data (Load or Store). A program can test for zero set or cleared by using BEQ or BNE respectively.

3. **Setting the break (B) flag** using the BRK command causes what is known as an interrupt. More will be said about interrupts in Chapter 11. Using a BRK command will cause your machine language program to stop and the computer to jump indirect on the contents of $FFFE and $FFFF. These ROM addresses hold the address of a break routine which will return you to BASIC. Using the BRK

command is a very effective way of debugging a program. By inserting this command into your program at specific points, you will be able to trace (by whether the program stops or hangs) how far a program is getting before it is doing the wrong thing. This instruction gives you a chance to stop a program and test its variables in memory to see if they are what you would expect at this point in the program. Use the BRK command within one of the programs from Chapter 7 to practise using it as a debugging tool.

4. **The interrupt (I) flag** may be set or cleared using SEI and CLI respectively. When set, the interrupt flag will disable certain types of interrupts from occurring (see Chapter 11).

5. **The decimal (D) flag** may be set or cleared using the SED and CLD commands respectively. When the decimal flag is set, the microprocessor goes into decimal or BCD mode. BCD stands for Binary Coded Decimal and is a method of representing decimal numbers within the computer's memory. In the BCD representation, hexadecimal digits 0 – 9 are read as their decimal equivalents and the digits A – F have no meaning. In other words,

BCD REPRESENTATION

Binary	Hex	Decimal value of BCD
00000000	00	0
00000001	01	1
00000010	02	2
00000011	03	3
00000100	04	4
00000101	05	5
00000110	06	6
00000111	07	7
00001000	08	8
00001001	09	9
00010000	10	10
00010001	11	11
00100010	22	22
01000011	43	43
10011000	98	98

This shows that there are six possible codes between the values of 9 and 10 which are wasted.

In decimal mode the microprocessor automatically adds and subtracts BCD numbers, e.g.

Decimal Flag = 0	Decimal Flag = 1
17	17
+26	+26
3D	43

The problems with decimal mode are that it is wasteful of memory and it is very slow to use mathematically (apart from adds and subtracts). On the whole it is easier to use hex and convert for output, and so decimal mode is rarely used. Convert some of the programs in Chapter 5 to work in decimal mode and compare their output to normal calculations.

6. **The negative flag**. So far we have said that the only numbers that could be held within a single byte were those between 0 and 255. We have talked about having to deal with numbers bigger than 255 by using two bytes, but we have not mentioned anything about numbers less than zero. We have used them briefly without realising it back in Chapter 6. We have seen from our use of numbers from 0 — 255 to represent anything from numbers to addresses, from characters to BCD numbers, that the microprocessor will behave the same no matter how we use these numbers. The memory might be a character or an address or an instruction, but if we add one to it the microprocessor will not care what it is we are representing. It will just do it blindly. In Chapter 6 we took our number between 0 and 255 and chose to use it as the value of a relative branch; we chose $00 to $7F as a forward (positive) and $80 to $FF as a backward (negative) branch. This numbering system is purely arbitrary but, as it turns out, it is mathematically sound to use it for representing positive and negative numbers. The system we use is called Two's Complement Arithmetic. We can use the table in Appendix 00 to convert between normal numbers and two's complement numbers, looking for the number in decimal in the centre and finding the correct two's complement hex value on the outside. Mathematically, we take the complement of the binary number (all 1's become 0's and all 0's become 1's) and then add 1, e.g.

COMPLEMENT

$$3 = 0\ 0\ 0\ 0\ 0\ 0\ 1\ 1 \rightarrow \boxed{1|1|1|1|1|1|0|0}$$
$$+1$$
$$= \boxed{1|1|1|1|1|1|0|1} = FD = -3$$

Using this representation, you will see that any byte whose value is greater than 127 (with its high bit, bit 7, turned on) represents a negative number, and any value less than 128 (high bit turned off) represents a positive number.

1 X X X X X X X — NEGATIVE
0 X X X X X X X — POSITIVE

The negative flag in the status register is automatically set (like the zero flag) if any number used as a result of an operation, a comparison or a transfer, is negative. Since the microprocessor cannot tell if a value it is dealing with represents a number or a character or anything else, it always sets the negative flag, if the high bit of the byte being used is set.

In other words, the negative flag is always a copy of bit 7 (the high bit) of the result of an operation.

Since the high bit of the byte is a sign bit (representing the sign of the number) we are left with only seven bits to store the actual number. With seven bits you can represent any number between 0 and 127 but, since 0 = −0, on the negative side we add one. So two's complement numbers can represent any number from −128 to +127 using one byte.

Let's try some mathematics using our new numbering system.

Two's Complement Binary   Decimal value

Positive + Positive (no different no normal)
```
  00000111                          +  7
+ 00001001                          ++ 9
```
```
  00010000                          16  C = 0 V = 0 N = 0
```

Positive + Negative (negative result)
```
  00000111                          +  7
+ 11110100                          + −12
```
```
  11111011                          −  5  C = 0 V = 0 N = 1
```

Positive + Negative (positive result)
```
   00000111                         +  7
 + 11111101                         + − 3
```
```
(1)00000100                         +  4  C = 1 V = 0 N = 0
```

Positive + Positive (answer greater than 127)
```
  01110011                          115
+ 00110001                          + 49
```
```
  10100100                          −92  C = 0 V = 1 N = 1
```

NOTE: this answer is **wrong!**

Two's complement numbering seems to handle positive and negative numbers well, except in our last example. We said previously that two's complement could only hold numbers from −128 to +127. The answer to our question should have been 164. As in Chapter 3, to hold a number bigger than 255 we needed two bytes, here also we must use two bytes. In normal binary a carry from bit 7 (the high bit) into the high byte was done through the carry. In two's complement we have seven bits and a sign bit so the high bit is bit 6. The microprocessor, not knowing we are using two's complement arithmetic, has as usual 'carried' bit 6 into bit 7. To enable us to correct this, it has set the overflow flag to tell us that this has happened.

7. **The overflow flag.** This flag is set by a carry from bit 6 to bit 7.

7 6 5 4 3 2 1 0

e.g. | 0 | 1 | 1 | 1 | 1 | 1 | 1 | 1 | + | 0 | 0 | 0 | 0 | 0 | 0 | 0 | 1 | = | 1 | 0 | 0 | 0 | 0 | 0 | 0 | 0 |

     127   +   1   =   128

The major use of the overflow flag is in signalling the accidental changing of sign caused by an 'overflow' using two's complement arithmetic. To correct for this accidental change of signs, the sign bit (bit 7) must be complemented (inverted) and a one carried on to a high byte if necessary.

This would make our previously wrong result of −92 (10100100) become 1 x 128 (high byte) + 36 (00100100). 128 + 36 = 164 which is the correct answer.

A program can test for the negative flag being set or cleared using BMI (Branch on Minus) or BPL (Branch on Plus) respectively.

A program can test for the overflow flag being set or cleared using BVS (Branch on Overflow Set) or BVC (Branch on Overflow Clear) respectively. The overflow flag can be cleared using the CLV command.

Chapter 9   SUMMARY

1. The microprocessor contains a special purpose register, the processor status code register.

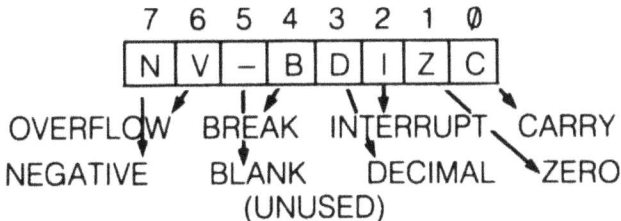

7 6 5 4 3 2 1 0

| N | V | − | B | D | I | Z | C |

OVERFLOW   BREAK   INTERRUPT   CARRY

NEGATIVE   BLANK   DECIMAL   ZERO
(UNUSED)

2. CARRY — SEC, CLC

         BCS, BCC

        Set if carry condition occurs.

3. ZERO — BEQ, BNE
   Set if a result or transfer = 0.

4. BRK is an instruction which sets the break flag and halts the microprocessor (useful for debugging purposes).

5. INTERRUPT — SEI, CLI

   See Chapters 11, 12.

6. DECIMAL — SED, CLD

   Sets decimal mode. Addition and subtraction are done using BCD (Binary Coded Decimal).

7. Two's complement numbering represents numbers from -128 to 127.

   negative X = (complement (X)) + 1

8. NEGATIVE — flag set if bit 7 of result is turned on ($=1$)

   BMI, BPL

9. OVERFLOW — set on two's complement carry
   CLV
   BVS, BVC

Chapter 10
Logical Operators and Bit Manipulators

Changing bits within memory

In this chapter we will be looking at a group of instructions unlike any others we have looked at previously, yet they are absolutely fundamental to the workings of a computer. They are the 'logical' or 'Boolean' operations. They are the commands AND (Logical AND), ORA (Logical OR), and EOR (Logical Exclusive OR). These functions can be built up using fairly simple circuitry, and almost all functions of the computer are built up by series of these circuits. The logical operations of these circuits are available to us through these instructions and it is this, and not the hardware, with which we will concern ourselves in this chapter.

We know that bytes of memory and the registers are made up of groups of eight bits:

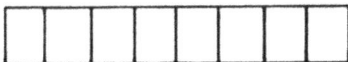

To explain the functions of these instructions, we look at their operation on one bit and then assume that this operation is done on all eight bits at once. A logical operator is like a mathematical function in that it takes in two pieces of data and puts out its result as one, e.g.

$$4 + 5 = 9$$

In this case however the data coming in is going to be single bit values, either 1's or 0's. To define a logical function we draw up a 'truth' table showing all possible inputs and the associated output.

63

INPUT 1 / INPUT 2	∅	1
∅	OUTPUT FOR ∅, ∅	OUTPUT FOR ∅, 1
1	OUTPUT FOR 1, ∅	OUTPUT FOR 1, 1

The logical AND

The first instruction we will deal with is the AND instruction. This performs a logical AND of the accumulator and the specified memory, leaving the result in A. The result of a logical AND is 1 if input is a 1 **and** input 2 is a 1. The truth table for this function looks like:

AND

MEMORY / ACCUMULATOR	∅	1
∅	∅	∅
1	∅	1

When extended to an eight bit byte this means that:

```
        ∅ 1 1 ∅ 1 ∅ 1 1
AND     1 ∅ 1 1 1 ∅ 1 ∅
  =     ∅ ∅ 1 ∅ 1 ∅ 1 ∅
```

The zero flag is set if the result = ∅, i.e. if there are no coincident ones in the bits of the two bytes used.

The AND instruction is useful in creating a 'mask' to turn off certain bits within a byte. Suppose, within a byte of any value, we wish to turn off the 3rd, 5th and 6th bits. We would create a 'mask' with only the 3rd, 5th and 6th bits turned **off** and AND this with the byte in question.

```
                7 6 5 4 3 2 1 ∅
Mask =          1 ∅ ∅ 1 ∅ 1 1 1      = $97

AND   #$97
```

would turn off the 3rd, 5th and 6th bits of whatever was in the accumulator.

The logical OR

The second instruction we will look at is the ORA instruction. This does a logical OR of the accumulator with the specified memory leaving the result in the accumulator.

The OR function outputs a 1 if input 1 is a 1 **or** input 2 is a 1. The truth table for this function looks like:

OR	ACCUMULATOR \ MEMORY	0	1
	0	0	1
	1	1	1

When extended to an eight bit byte this means that:

	0	1	0	1	0	0	1	0
ORA	0	0	1	1	1	0	1	0
=	0	1	1	1	1	0	1	0

The zero flag is set if both bytes are used and hence the result is zero.

The ORA instruction is useful for turning on certain bits within a byte using the masking technique.

Suppose we want to turn on the 2nd, 3rd and 7th bits within a byte. We would use a mask with only the 2nd, 3rd and 7th bits turned **on**.

```
            7 6 5 4 3 2 1 0
Mask  =     1 0 0 0 1 1 0 0   =  $8C
ORA  #$8C
```

would turn on the 2nd, 3rd and 7th bits of whatever was in the accumulator.

The logical exclusive OR

The last of the logical operators is the EOR. This does a logical exclusive — OR of the accumulator and memory leaving the result in A. The exclusive — OR function outputs a 1 if input is a 1 **or** input 2 is a 1 **but** not if both are a 1. The truth table for this function looks like:

EOR	ACCUMULATOR \ MEMORY	0	1
	0	0	1
	1	1	0

When extended to an eight bit byte the exclusive — OR produces:

|1|0|1|1|1|0|0|1|

EOR |1|0|1|0|0|1|0|1|

= |0|0|0|1|1|1|0|0|

The exclusive — OR is used to complement (invert) certain bits within a byte using masking.

To invert the 1st, 2nd and 4th bits of a byte we would use a mask with those bits turned **on**.

7 6 5 4 3 2 1 0

Mask = |0|0|0|1|0|1|1|0| = $16

EOR #$16

would invert those bits of the accumulator.

Type the following program in, to test these instructions:

    LDA #$CA
    AND #$9F
    STA $03
    LDA #$A2
    ORA #$84
    EOR $03
    STA $03
    BRK

Program summary

Line 1		A = $CA	11001010
Line 2 AND $9F		A = $8A	10001010
Line 3	STORE	A = $03	10001010
Line 4		A = $A2	10100010
Line 5 ORA $84		A = #A6	10100110
Line 6 EOR $03		A = $2C	00101100

ENTER and RUN this program

and verify the results with those we have reached.

The bit instruction

There is a useful instruction in the 7501 instruction set which does an interesting set of tests and comparisons. We discussed in Chapter 6 how the CMP command did a subtraction setting the status flags but not storing the result. Similarly BIT (compare memory bits with the accumulator) does a logical AND of A and memory, setting only the Z flag as a result. The bit instruction also copies bit 7 into the negative flag and bit 6 into the overflow flag.

Rotating bits within a byte

We will now discuss four other bit manipulation instructions and some of their consequences. The first instruction we will look at is ASL (Arithmetic Shift Left). This instruction shifts all the bits in the specified byte left by one bit, introducing a zero at the low end and moving the high bit off into the carry flag.

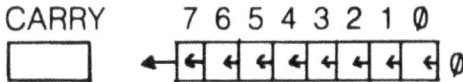

CARRY 　　　 7 6 5 4 3 2 1 0

```
┌───┐    ┌─┬─┬─┬─┬─┬─┬─┬─┐
│   │ ◄──│◄│◄│◄│◄│◄│◄│◄│◄│ 0
└───┘    └─┴─┴─┴─┴─┴─┴─┴─┘
```

hence

C = ? |0|1|0|1|0|1|0|1|

becomes

C = 0 |1|0|1|0|1|0|1|0|

and

C = ? |1|0|1|1|0|1|1|0|

becomes

C = 1 |0|1|1|0|1|1|0|0|

Back in Chapter 3 when we explained hex and binary we mentioned that each bit had the value of $2^{position-1}$

i.e. |128|64|32|16|8|4|2|1|

You will notice that the value of each box is two times the value of the box to the right of it, hence:

00000001 x 2 = 00000010 and
00001000 x 2 = 00010000

and furthermore

00111001 x 2 = 01110010

The operation required to multiply any byte by two is the operation performed by the ASL instruction.

To use our examples from before:

C = ? 01010101 ($55)×2 → C = 0 10101010 ($AA)

and

C = ? 10110110 ($B6)×2 → C = 1 01101100 ($6C + CARRY)

Type in the following program:

```
LDA #$0A
ASL A
STA $03
BRK
```

Use the .M command to examine location $03.

NOTE: this is different to implied addressing because ASL may be used on data from memory.

We can use this instruction to multiply a number by any power of 2 (1, 2, 4, 8. . .). To use the previous program to multiply by eight instead of two, insert the following two lines:

```
ASL A
ASL A
```

after the first line.

Rotation with carry

As with our addition routines, we may find we want to multiply numbers greater than 255 (two or more byte numbers). To do this there is a shift command which uses the carry on the input end of the shift as well as the output end:

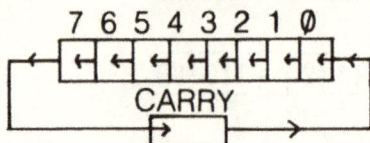

The instruction to do this is ROL (Rotate One bit Left). To do a two byte multiply by four, type the following lines:

```
LDA #$17
STA $03
ROL $03
ROL $03
BRK
```

We are multiplying the two byte number $170A by four.

NOTE: 1. To avoid swapping registers we have used ROL absolute which stores its result back in memory.

2. We have rotated both bytes once and then rotated both again. Rotating the low byte twice and then the high byte twice would not work, because the high bit from the low byte would be lost when the carry was used in the second ASL.

ENTER and RUN the program.

Put together the high and low bytes of the answer and check that it equals four times our original number.

Rotating to the right

LSR and ROR are the equivalent instructions to ASL and ROL, except that they shift the bits in the opposite direction.

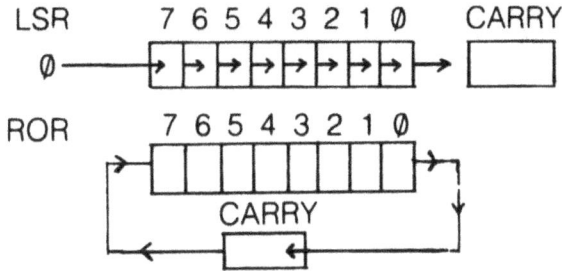

Just as their opposites can be thought of as multiplications by two, so these can be thought of as division by two, and can be similarly extended to multi-byte arithmetic. After division, the number left in the byte is the integer part of the result and the bits which have been shifted out represent the remainder, e.g.

$1D ÷ $08 = 3   remainder 5

```
        00011101   = 29    remainder
LSR  ÷ 2
        00001110   = 14    →  1 = 1
LSR  ÷ 4
        00000111   =  7    → 01 = 1
LSR  ÷ 8
        00000011   =  3    → 101 = 5
```

NOTE: Just because the shift and rotate instructions can be used for arithmetic, do not forget their use for shifting bits, e.g. shifting into carry for testing.

Clever multiplication

We have said that by shifting bits we can multiply by any power of 2 (1, 2, 4, 8 . . ., 128). These are the same values that represent each bit within a byte. We have shown in Chapter 3 that by adding these values we can produce any number between 0 and 255.

If we then multiply by each of these values and add the results, this process is equivalent to multiplying by any value from 0 to 255, e.g.

```
$16 x $59 = 00010110 x $59
          = 00010000 x $59
          + 00000100 x $59
          + 00000010 x $59
     = 16 x $59 + 4 x $59 + 2 x $59
```

which we know how to work out from our previous multiplication.

This is the algorithm we will use in our generalised multiplication routine. We will rotate (multiply by two) one number, and add it to the total, for each bit turned on in the other byte, e.g.

```
10110 x $59
  rotate   $59                                    1 0 1 1 [0]
  rotate   $59      add to total                  1 0 1 [1] 0
  rotate   $59      add to total                  1 0 [1] 1 0
  rotate   $59                                    1 [0] 1 1 0
  rotate   $59      add to total                  [1] 0 1 1 0
```

For simplicity's sake, our generalised multiplication routine will only handle results less than 255.

To multiply $1B by $09 type:

```
         LDA #$1B
         STA $03
         LDA #$09
         STA $03
         LDA #$00
         ROR $04
L70      ROL $04
         LSR $03
         BCC L120
         CLC
         ADC $04
L120     BNE L70
         STA $05
         BRK
```

Program summary

lines 1 - 6	initialise values to be multiplied and the total to 0. The ROR followed by ROL has no effect the first time through but only the ROL is within the loop.
line 7	except for the first time through, this multiplies one of the numbers (2) by two each time around the loop.
lines 8 - 9	rotates the other number (1) bit by bit into the carry, and then tests the carry to see if the other number (2) should be added this time around the loop. If the carry is clear, the possibility that the number (1) has been shifted completely through (= 0 — Multiplication is completed) is tested — line 12.
lines 10 - 11	add to the total (in A) the number (2) which is being multiplied by two each time around the loop.
line 12	if the branch on line 9 was taken, this will test for the end of multiplication (number (1) = 0 shifted completely

through). If the branch on line 9 was not taken, this branch on not equal will always be true because we are adding a number (2) greater than zero to a total which will not be greater than 255.

lines 13 - 14   END.

NOTE: this multiplication routine is much more efficient than the one given in Chapter 7. By that method we would have had to loop at least nine times, whereas with this, had we swapped and used 9 as number (1) and $1B as number (2), we would have only looped four times (number of bits needed to make 9 — 1001).

Type:

WATCH   (address ? 336)
ENTER
RUN

and verify the results.

Now change the numbers used to perform a different calculation (make sure the answer <256), e.g.

10 A906   LDA #$06
30 A925   LDA #$25
ENTER and RUN

with these values and again verify the results for yourself.

Chapter 10   SUMMARY

1. AND

	0	1
0	0	0
1	0	1

most often used to mask **off** bits.

2. ORA

	0	1
0	0	1
1	1	1

most often used to mask **on** bits.

3. EOR (exclusive or)

	0	1
0	0	1
1	1	0

most often used to mask **invert** bits.

4. BIT   performs AND without storing the result.

Z is set or cleared
N becomes bit 7
V becomes bit 6

5. ASL

7 6 5 4 3 2 1 0   Arithmetic Shift Left

```
[      ] ←— [←|←|←|←|←|←|←|←] —0
 CARRY
```

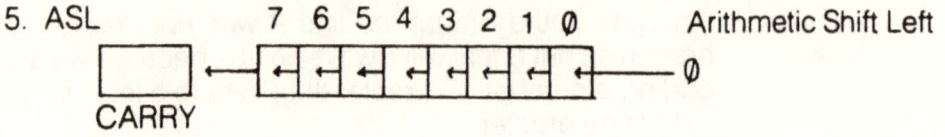

most often used to multiply by 2.

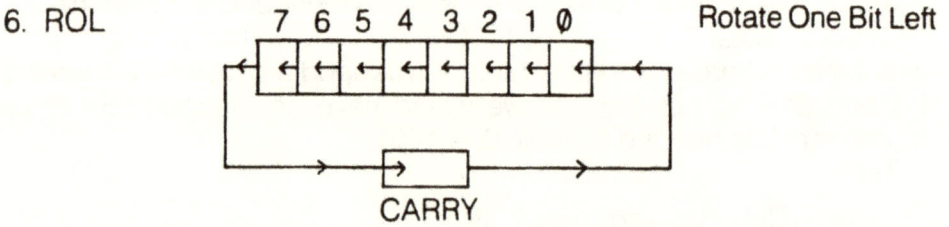

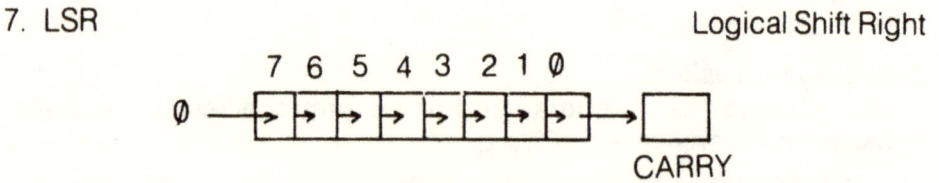

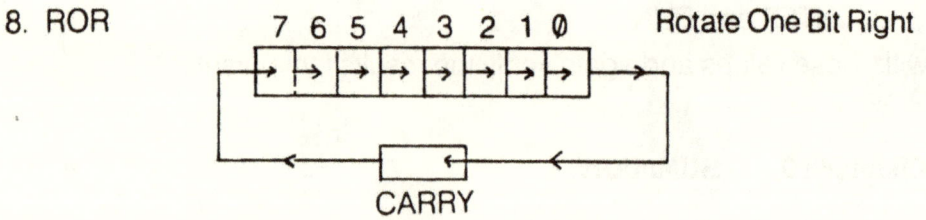

6. ROL

7 6 5 4 3 2 1 0   Rotate One Bit Left

```
←[←|←|←|←|←|←|←|←]←
         [→]
        CARRY
```

7. LSR

Logical Shift Right

7 6 5 4 3 2 1 0

```
0 —→[→|→|→|→|→|→|→|→]—→[      ]
                        CARRY
```

8. ROR

7 6 5 4 3 2 1 0   Rotate One Bit Right

```
[→|→|→|→|→|→|→|→]—→
        [←]
       CARRY
```

72

Chapter 11
Details of Program Control

The program counter

We have talked a lot about the different operations that the microprocessor can perform, but we have said very little about how it goes about those tasks. This is perfectly alright, because in most cases we don't need to know. In one case, however, knowing how the microprocessor is operating leads us into a whole new list of commands and a powerful area of the microprocessor's capabilities.

The microprocessor contains a special purpose, two byte register called the Program Counter (PC), whose sole job is to keep track of where the next instruction is coming from in memory. In other words, the program counter contains the address of the next byte to be loaded into the microprocessor and used as a command.

If we think of our post office boxes again, each holding either an instruction (opcode) or the data/address it acts upon (operand), this is what our program looks like, e.g.

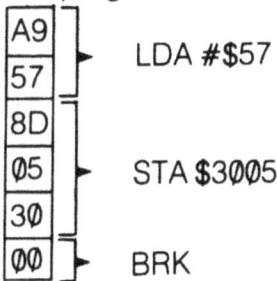

To 'run' our post office box program, we would go through each box in turn and act on the data within each box. Now imagine there was a large clock type counter showing a box address which we looked at to know which box to find. Normally this counter would go up one by one, taking the next byte in order. However, if it wanted us to move to a new area of the boxes, it would just flash up the address of the next instruction it wanted us to find. This is exactly how the JMP command operates.

Storing into the program counter

The instruction JMP $address only loads the two byte $address into the program counter, the next instruction is then loaded from memory at that address, and a JMP has been executed.

NOTE: the branch instructions add or subtract from the program counter in a similar way, thereby creating a 'relative' jump.

The program counter and subroutines

If it were possible to store the program counter just before doing a JMP and changing it to a new address, we would later be able to return to the same place in memory by reloading that stored piece of memory back into the program counter. In other words, if we had noticed that the post office box counter was about to change, and we noted down the address it showed (our current address) before it changed, we would at some future stage place that back on the counter and return to where we had left off.

This, of course, is a subroutine structure, e.g.

```
10 PRINT "HELLO WORLD"
20 GOSUB 100
30 PRINT "I'M FINE"
40 END
100 PRINT "HOW ARE YOU?"
110 RETURN
```

would print:

```
HELLO WORLD
HOW ARE YOU?
I'M FINE
```

We said at the beginning of the book that a machine language program can be thought of as a subroutine called from BASIC using the SYS command.

You can also create subroutines from within a machine language program. They are called using the JSR (Jump to Subroutine) command. As when called from BASIC, to return from a machine language subroutine you use the RTS (Return From Subroutine) command.

```
2000 LDX #$00  ┐
2002 JSR $2009  │
2005 INX        ├─ controlling portion
2006 BNE $2002  │   of program
2008 BRK        ┘

2009 LDY #$03  ┐
200B STY $0C00  │
200E DEY        ├─ subroutine
200F BNE $200B  │
2011 RTS        ┘
```

Remember that this program will go extremely fast.

It is good programming style to use subroutines for two major reasons. Firstly, it is easy to locate and fix errors within subroutines. They can be tested and fixed independently of the rest of the program. Secondly, by using subroutines it is possible to build up a 'library' of useful subroutines, e.g. sprite movers, screen clearers, byte finders etc. which may be added as a subroutine to any program.

We have said that the return address of the subroutine is stored away but we have not said anything about **how** it is stored. We want some sort of filing system to store this address which will give us a number of necessary features.

The stack control structure

Firstly, it must be flexible and easy to use. Secondly, we would like to be able to provide for the possibility that a subroutine will be called from within a subroutine (called from within a subroutine, called from within . . .). In this case we have to use a system which will not only remember a return address for each of the subroutines called, but will have to remember which is the correct return address for each subroutine. The system which we use to store the addresses on a data structure is called a 'stack'. A stack is a LIFO structure (Last In First Out). When an RTS is reached, we want the last address put on the stack to be used as a return address for the subroutine.

Imagine the stack to be one of those spikes that people sometimes keep messages on.

Every time you see a JSR instruction, you copied down the return address onto a scrap of paper from the post office box counter. As soon as you had done this, you spiked the piece of paper on the stack. If you came across another JSR you merely repeated the process. Now when you come across an RTS, the only piece of paper you can take off the spike (stack) is the top one. The others are all blocked by those on top of them. This top piece of paper will always contain the correct return address for the subroutine you are returning from (that which was most recently called).

Subroutines and the stack

The JSR and RTS commands do this automatically using the system stack. The stack sits in memory from $100 to $1FF (Page 1) and grows downwards. (Imagine the spike turned upside down). This makes no difference to its operation. The top of the stack (or actually the bottom) is marked by a special purpose register within the microprocessor called the Stack Pointer (SP). When a JSR is done, the two byte program counter is put on the stack and the stack pointer (SP) is decremented by two (a two byte address is put on).

BEFORE

Program Counter

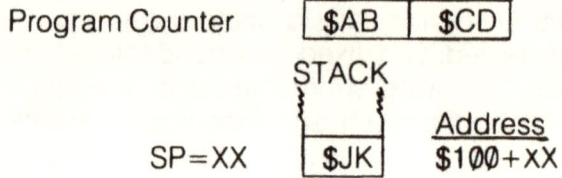

AFTER (JSR $PQMN)

Program Counter

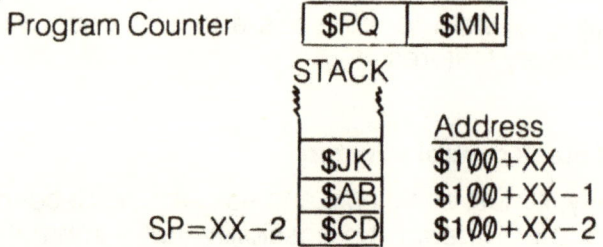

An RTS takes the top two bytes off the stack and returns them to the program counter. The stack pointer is incremented by two.

BEFORE

Program Counter

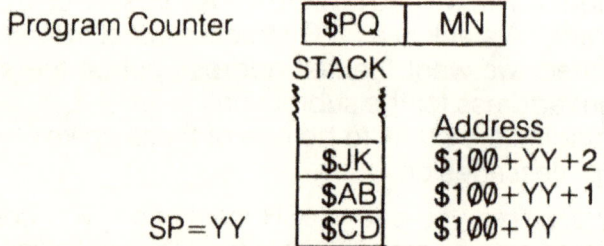

AFTER   (RTS)

Program Counter

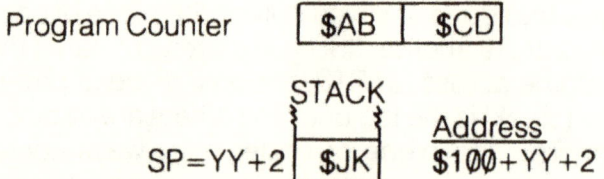

DUMP memory from $100 to $200 to have a look at the stack memory.

One major advantage of the stack is that it can also be used to store data by using the instructions PHA (Push Accumulator onto the Stack) and PLA (Pull Accumulator off the Stack) respectively to put the contents of the accumulator on and off the stack.

WARNING: make sure you put things on and off the stack in the correct order.

If you use the RTS while there is extra data on the top of the stack, the

RTS will return to an address made up of the two top bytes of the stack whatever they are.

Let us use these instructions to test the operation of the stack. Type:

```
        JSR L40
        INC $D020
        RTS
L40     PLA
        TAX
        PLA
        STX $03
        STA $04
        PHA
        TXA
        PHA
        BRK
```

Program summary

Line 1	JSR — return address (address of next instruction is placed on the stack). (Actually it points to the byte **before** the next instruction because the PC is incremented each time before a byte is 'fetched' from memory.)
Line 2	increments screen border colour (see Appendix 6) just to show that the program has returned satisfactorily. satisfactorily.
Line 3	END
Lines 4 - 6	take the top two bytes of the stack $03, $04.
Lines 7 - 8	store them low byte/high byte.
Lines 9 - 11	return bytes to stack IN CORRECT ORDER
Line 12	END of Subroutine.

ENTER and RUN this program. Examine the location $04. Put the results together and compare them against the expected address.

The two instructions TSX (Transfer SP into X) and TXS (Transfer X into SP) are available to do direct manipulations on the SP. Write a program with a subroutine within a subroutine, both of which save the SP in memory (via X) to see the change in SP when a subroutine is called and when an RTS is executed.

Interrupts

Although it is felt that a full explanation of interrupts is unwarranted in a book of this nature, you should at least be aware of what they are, and the role that they play in the operating system. An interrupt, in general, is sent to the computer's microprocessor by an external hardware device.

Interrupts are used primarily to alert the computer to the fact that something is going on in the outside world, which might require its attention. For example, every sixtieth of a second an interrupt is sent, to remind the computer to carry out the update of the 'jiffy' clock and to read the keyboard.

When an interrupt is generated, the computer stops what it is currently doing and rushes off to a separate routine, which is designed to handle the interrupt. When the computer has finished the interrupt routine, it automatically returns to where it was interrupted from. There are several types of interrupt that may occur, and so there are several of these 'interrupt routines' that the computer may be sent to. The absolute addresses of these routines can be found from the following two byte vectors.

$fffe-$ffff   This vector points to the routine which handles what are knows an I.R.Q. (interrupt request) interrupts. This form of interrupt is generated by such sources as the clock which generates an interrupt every sixtieth of a second. BRK interrupts (software) also pass through to the program pointed to by this vector. Interrupts that pass through this vector may be prevented with the use of the SEI (set interrupt disable) instruction, and re-enabled using the CLI (clear interrupt disable) instruction. For this reason, interrupts that use this vector are often known as 'maskable' interrupts.

$fffa-$fffb   This vector points to the routine that handles N.M.I.s (non-maskable interrupts). These forms of interrupts cannot be disabled. The C16 does not make use of non-maskable interrupts.

NOTE: It is posssible to trap the computer before it goes to its I.R.Q. interrupt routine, sending it instead to a routine that you may have written yourself. This is made possible due to the fact that the computer uses another vector, which is situated in R.A.M., at locations $0314 and $0315, to get to its interrupt routine. This address may be changed to the start of your own interrupt handling routine. At this stage, however, it is recommended that you do NOT change the vector at these locations before consulting other material which covers interrupts more extensively. In the event that this vector is changed incorrectly the computer may 'hang', requiring the turning off of your computer, or the depression of the reset switch.

Chapter 11   SUMMARY

1. Program Counter (PC) points to the next byte in memory to be used as an instruction.

2. JMP stores address in PC.

3. Branches add or subtract from PC.

4. JSR stores PC on stack and stores new address in PC (subroutine).

5. RTS takes the top two bytes off stack stores in PC (return address).

6. The stack can only have things put on at one end. They can only be taken off from the same end in the same order they were put on.

7. The stack pointer keeps track of the 'top' of the stack.

$$RTS \Rightarrow SP=SP+2$$
$$JSR \Rightarrow SP=SP-2$$

8. PHA, PLA store and retrieve the accumulator from the stack. Be sure to take things off the stack in the same order they went on.

9. TXS, TSX transfer contents between the stack pointer and X.

10. BRK   PC   →Stack (2 bytes)
    Status byte   →Stack
    Contents of
    (FFFE,FFFF)   →PC

11. PHP, PLP push and pull a processor status word onto the stack.

12. Interrupts come from chips external to the microprocessor
    PC   →Stack (2 bytes)
    Status byte   →Stack
    (FFFE,FFFF)   →PC

They are handled by ROM handling routines.

Chapter 12
Commodore 16 Kernal

Concepts of Kernal and Operating System

A microprocessor, no matter how large its instruction set is and no matter how fast it can run, will get nowhere without a well-knit piece of software that supervises it. This supervisory program is known as an OPERATING SYSTEM. The operating system accepts what you type on the keyboard; echoes it on the monitor; prints an error message if it does not understand what you typed; executes your command if it makes sense; loads a program from disk drive if necessary; prints something on the printer if required ... In other words, the operating system co-ordinates and manages all resources of the computer to be at your service.

The operating system has a large collection of routines that perform system initializations, memory management and all kinds of input/output. These routines are usually highly hardware dependent which means different routines have to be written for different devices. From a user point of view, you want to be able to use these routines without worrying about what hardware you are dealing with. Most microcomputer manufacturers prepare a list of callable system routines with their addresses and methods of calling. The problem arises when a later version of the operating system is released; all these entry points will be different. Old software which made use of these routines is no longer compatible.

Commodore 16 has solved this problem by storing all the entry points of the supported system routines in a Jump Table called KERNAL. This jump table is located on the last page of memory, in the KERNAL ROM. The entries of this table are well documented and will remain unchanged in future ROM releases. Any individual system routine can be modified and relocated inside the ROM. However, such a change will be 'transparent' to the user program as long as the jump pointer in the KERNAL has been updated.

Example:

$FFC6 JMP ($031C)   JSR $FFC6   JMP ($031C) $FFC6

$ED18

RTS $XXXX

Application
Program
                                                 RTS

ROM 3.5   ROM X.X

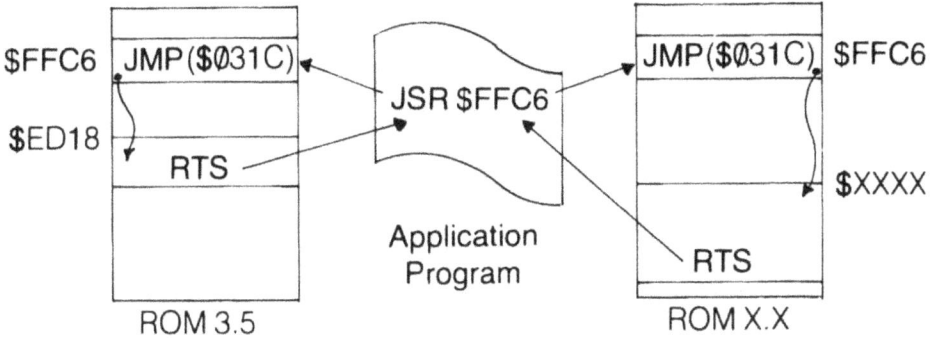

The application program will run just as well on both ROM versions.

Some useful Kernal routines

Routine	Address	Function	Preparatory Routines	Communications Registers	Registers Affected
User Interface					
1. CHRIN	$FFCF	Input 1 Character (from keyboard)	—	.A = input character	.X, .Y
2. CHROUT	$FFD2	Output 1 Character (to Screen)	—	.A = output character	—
3. GETIN	$FFE4	Get 1 Character from Keyboard Queue	—	.A = character removed =0 if none	.X, .Y
4. PLOT	$FFF0	Read/Set Cursor Position	—	C flag= 1 read =0 set .X = row(0-24) .Y = column(0-39)	.A
storage I/O					
5. SETLFS	$FFBA	Set Up Logical File No. First Address (Device No.) and Second Address (Command) of Device	—	.A = logical file no. .X = device no. .Y = command = $FF if no command	—
6. SETNAM	$FFBD	Set Up File Name	—	.A = length of filename .X = filename address (low) .Y = filename address (high)	—
7. LOAD	$FFD5	Load/Verify Memory from Device	SETLFS SETNAM	.A = 0 load = 1 verify	.X, .Y
8. SAVE	$FFD8	Save Memory to Device	SETLFS SETNAM	.A = page-zero address of start SAVE pointer .X = end SAVE pointer address (low) .Y = end SAVE pointer address (high)	

Using Kernal routines

For you to use the KERNAL routines, you must:
- — find out the right one to use and its entry point address
- — call preparatory routine, if necessary
- — pass parameters in communication registers
- — call the routine
- — handle any return error (indicated by Carry Flag set)
- — save and restore registers affected by the routine, if necessary.

1. CHRIN — INPUT 1 CHARACTER (FROM KEYBOARD)

When this routine is initially called, the cursor will blink and input a line of characters terminated with a carriage return. The routine will return with the first character in .A. Subsequent calls will retrieve the characters already input one by one. Detection of a carriage return means the whole input line has been retrieved. A subsequent call will initiate the cursor blinking and line input again.

2. CHROUT — OUTPUT 1 CHARACTER (TO SCREEN)

A character whose ASCII value is in the .A is printed on the screen and the cursor advances.

3. GETIN — GET 1 CHARACTER FROM KEYBOARD QUEUE

Any key pressed on the keyboard is detected by the system IRQ interrupt handler. Its ASCII code will be stored in a keyboard buffer queue which can hold up to 10 characters. When called, this routine will remove the first character from the queue. If there is no character in the queue, a byte zero will be returned in the .A.

4. PLOT — READ/SET CURSOR POSITION

This routine can read/set the current cursor position when called with the Carry Flag set/clear accordingly. .X stores the row number (0-24) and .Y stores the column number (0-39).

5. SETLFS — SET LOGICAL FILE NUMBER, FIRST AND SECOND ADDRESS OF DEVICE

This routine assigns a logical file number to a physical device (device number 0-31). The secondary address or command of the device is also declared here. There are a number of reserved device numbers for the Commodore 16:

Device number	Device
0	Keyboard
1	Cassette
2	RS-232 Device
3	Screen
4	Serial Bus Printer
5	Serial Bus Disk Drive

.A is used to pass the logical file number .X the device number and .Y the command. If no command is required, put $FF in .Y.

6. SETNAM — SET UP FILE NAME

This routine sets up a file name for the LOAD or SAVE routine. .A is used to pass the length of the file name and .X and .Y contain the address of the file name (.X = low order, .Y = high order address). If no file name is necessary, .A stores a zero showing a file name of null length.

7. LOAD — LOAD/VERIFY MEMORY FROM DEVICE

When called with a zero in .A, this routine loads a file from device into memory. When called with a one in .A, this routine verifies a file from device against the corresponding contents in the memory.

8. SAVE — SAVE MEMORY TO DEVICE

This routine saves a contiguous portion of memory onto a device file. The start address of the memory to be saved is stored in a page-zero pointer. The .A is used to pass the page-zero address of this start pointer. The .X and .Y are used to pass the end address (in low, high order).

Chapter 12 SUMMARY

1. The KERNAL in ROM handles the computer's contact with the outside world.
2. KERNAL routines will be upwardly compatible with later ROM releases.

APPENDICES

Introduction to the Appendices

We have provided you with charts and tables of useful information necessary for machine code programming on the Commodore 16. The information presented will stand as a useful reference long after you have left 'beginner' status but until then these tables can be used by the beginner. We have provided explanations and occasionally examples of the most useful parts of the tables. Those that have no accompanying explanation are really beyond the scope of this book and are included for interest's sake, as well as to give you a handy reference and a start towards more complex and intricate programming in the future.

Appendix 1

75Ø1 Instruction Codes

These tables should be a constant reference while writing machine code or assembly code programs. There is a list of every instruction with a description, available addressing modes, instruction format, number of bytes used, the hex code for the instruction, and a list of the status flags changed as a result of the instruction.

75Ø1 Microprocessor Instructions in alphabetical order

ADC	Add Memory to Accumulator with Carry	LDA	Load Accumulator with Memory
AND	"AND" Memory with Accumulator	LDX	Load Index X with Memory
ASL	Shift Left One Bit (Memory or Accumulator)	LDY	Load Index Y with Memory
		LSR	Shift Right one Bit (Memory or Accumulator)
BCC	Branch on Carry Clear		
BCS	Branch on Carry Set	NOP	No Operation
BEQ	Branch on Result Zero	ORA	"OR" Memory with Accumulator
BIT	Test Bits in Memory with Accumulator	PHA	Push Accumulator on Stack
		PHP	Push Processor Status on Stack
BMI	Branch on Result Minus	PLA	Pull Accumulator from Stack
BNE	Branch on Result not Zero	PLP	Pull Processor Status from Stack
BPL	Branch on Result Plus	ROL	Rotate One Bit Left (Memory or Accumulator)
BRK	Force Break		
BVC	Branch on Overflow Clear	ROR	Rotate One Bit Right (Memory or Accumulator)
BVS	Branch on Overflow Set		
CLC	Clear Carry Flag	RTI	Return from Interrupt
CLD	Clear Decimal Mode	RTS	Return from Subroutine
CLI	Clear Interrupt Disable Bit	SBC	Subtract Memory from Accumulator with Borrow
CLV	Clear Overflow flag		
CMP	Compare Memory and Accumulator	SEC	Set Carry Flag
		SED	Set Decimal Mode
CPX	Compare Memory and Index X	SEI	Set Interrupt Disable Status
CPY	Compare Memory and Index Y	STA	Store Accumulator in Memory
DEC	Decrement Memory by One	STX	Store Index X in Memory
DEX	Decrement Index X by One	STY	Store Index Y in Memory
DEY	Decrement Index Y by One	TAX	Transfer Accumulator to Index X
EOR	"Exclusive-Or" Memory with Accumulator	TAY	Transfer Accumulator to Index Y
		TSX	Transfer Stack Pointer to Index X
INC	Increment Memory by One	TXA	Transfer Index X to Accumulator
INX	Increment Index X by One	TXS	Transfer Index X to Stack Pointer
INY	Increment Index Y by One	TYA	Transfer Index Y to Accumulator
JMP	Jump to New Location		
JSR	Jump to New Location Saving Return Address		

75Ø1 Instruction Codes

Name Description	Addressing Mode	Assembly Language Form	No Bytes	HEX OP Code	Status Register
ADC Add memory to accumulator with carry	Immediate	ADC #Oper	2	69	N V - B D I Z C • • • •
	Zero Page	ADC Oper	2	65	
	Zero Page.X	ADC Oper.X	2	75	
	Absolute	ADC Oper	3	6D	
	Absolute.X	ADC Oper.X	3	7D	
	Absolute.Y	ADC Oper.Y	3	79	
	(Indirect X)	AND (Oper.X)	2	61	
	(Indirect).Y	ADC (Oper).Y	2	71	
AND "AND" memory with accumulator	Immediate	AND #Oper	2	29	N V - B D I Z C • •
	Zero Page	AND Oper	2	25	
	Zero Page.X	AND Oper.X	2	35	
	Absolute	AND Oper	3	2D	
	Absolute.X	AND Oper.X	3	3D	
	Absolute.Y	AND Oper.Y	3	39	
	(Indirect.X)	AND (Oper.X)	2	31	
	(Indirect).Y	AND (Oper.)Y	2	31	
ASL Shift left one bit (Memory or Accumulator)	Accumulator	ASL A	1	0A	N V - B D I Z C • • •
	Zero Page	ASL Oper	2	06	
	Zero Page.X	ASL Oper.X	2	16	
	Absolute	ASL Oper	3	0E	
	Absolute.X	ASL Oper.X	3	1E	

C←7 6 5 4 3 2 1 0←0

Name Description	Addressing Mode	Assembly Language Form	No Bytes	HEX OP Code	Status Register
BCC Branch on carry clear	Relative	BCC Oper	2	90	N V - B D I Z C
BCS Branch on carry set	Relative	BCS Oper	2	B0	N V - B D I Z C
BEQ Branch on result zero	Relative	BEQ Oper	2	F0	N V - B D I Z C
BIT Test bits in memory with accumulator	Zero Page	BIT Oper	1	24	N V - B D I Z C M M • 7 6
	Absolute	BIT Oper	3	2C	
BMI Branch on result minus	Relative	BMI Oper	2	30	N V - B D I Z C
BNE Branch on result not zero	Relative	BNE Oper	2	D0	N V - B D I Z C
BPL Branch on result plus	Relative	BPL oper	2	10	N V - B D I Z C
BRK Force Break	Implied	BRK	1	00	N V - B D I Z C 1 1
BVC Branch on overflow clear	Relative	BVC Oper	2	50	N V - B D I Z C

75Ø1 Instruction Codes

Name Description	Addressing Mode	Assembly Language Form	No Bytes	HEX OP Code	Status Register
BVS Branch on overflow set	Relative	BVS Oper	2	70	N V - B D I Z C
CLC Clear carry flag	Implied	CLC	1	18	N V - B D I Z C 0
CLD Clear decimal mode	Implied	CLD	1	D8	N V - B D I Z C 0
CLI Clear interrupt flag	Implied	CLI	1	58	N V - B D I Z C 0
CLV Clear overflow flag	Implied	CLV	1	B8	N V - B D I Z C 0
CMP Compare memory and accumulator	Immediate Zero Page Zero Page X Absolute Absolute X Absolute Y (Indirect X) (Indirect) Y	CMP #Oper CMP Oper CMP Oper X CMP Oper CMP Oper X CMP Oper Y CMP (Oper X) CMP (Oper) Y	2 2 2 3 3 3 2 2	C9 C5 D5 CD DD D9 C1 D1	N V - B D I Z C • • •
CPX Compare memory and index X	Immediate Zero Page Absolute	CPX #Oper CPX Oper CPX Oper	2 2 3	E0 E4 EC	N V - B D I Z C • • •
CPY Compare memory and index Y	Immediate Zero Page Absolute	CPY #Oper CPY Oper CPY Oper	2 2 3	C0 C4 CC	N V - B D I Z C • • •
DEC Decrement memory by one	Zero Page Zero Page X Absolute Absolute X	DEC Oper DEC Oper X DEC Oper DEC Oper X	2 2 3 3	C6 D6 CE DE	N V - B D I Z C • •
DEX Decrement index X by one	Implied	DEX	1	DA	N V - B D I Z C • •
DEY Decrement index Y by one	Implied	DEY	1	88	N V - B D I Z C • •

75Ø1 Instruction Codes

Name Description	Addressing Mode	Assembly Language Form	No Bytes	HEX OP Code	Status Register
EOR					N V · B D I Z C
"Exclusive Or" memory	Immediate	EOR #Oper	2	49	• •
with accumulator	Zero Page	EOR Oper	2	45	
	Zero Page X	EOR Oper X	2	55	
	Absolute	EOR Oper	3	4D	
	Absolute X	EOR Oper X	3	5D	
	Absolute Y	EOR Oper Y	3	59	
	(Indirect X)	EOR (Oper X)	2	41	
	(Indirect) Y	EOR (Oper) Y	2	51	
INC					N V · B D I Z C
Increment memory	Zero Page	INC Oper	2	E6	• •
by one	Zero Page X	INC Oper X	2	F6	
	Absolute	INC Oper	3	EE	
	Absolute X	INC Oper X	3	FE	
INX					N V · B D I Z C
Increment index X by one	Implied	INX	1	E8	• •
INY					N V · B D I Z C
Increment index Y by one	Implied	INY	1	C8	• •
JMP					N V · B D I Z C
Jump to new location	Absolute	JMP Oper	3	4C	
	Indirect	JMP (Oper)	3	6C	
JSR					N V · B D I Z C
Jump to new location saving return address	Absolute	JSR Oper	3	20	
LDA					N V · B D I Z C
Load accumulator	Immediate	LDA #Oper	2	A9	• •
with memory	Zero Page	LDA Oper	2	A5	
	Zero Page X	LDA Oper X	2	B5	
	Absolute	LDA Oper	3	AD	
	Absolute X	LDA Oper X	3	BD	
	Absolute Y	LDA Oper Y	3	B9	
	(Indirect X)	LDA (Oper X)	2	A1	
	(Indirect) Y	LDA (Oper) Y	2	B1	
LDX					N V · B D I Z C
Load index X	Immediate	LDX #Oper	2	A2	• •
with memory	Zero Page	LDX Oper	2	A6	
	Zero Page Y	LDX Oper Y	2	B6	
	Absolute	LDX Oper	3	AE	
	Absolute Y	LDX Oper Y	3	BE	
LDY					N V · B D I Z C
Load index Y	Immediate	LDY #Oper	2	A0	• •
with memory	Zero Page	LDY Oper	2	A4	
	Zero Page X	LDY Oper X	2	B4	
	Absolute	LDY Oper	3	AC	
	Absolute X	LDY Oper X	3	BC	

75Ø1 Instruction Codes

Name Description	Addressing Mode	Assembly Language Form	No Bytes	HEX OP Code	Status Register
BVS Branch on overflow set	Relative	BVS Oper	2	70	N V - B D I Z C
CLC Clear carry flag	Implied	CLC	1	18	N V - B D I Z C 0
CLD Clear decimal mode	Implied	CLD	1	D8	N V - B D I Z C 0
CLI Clear interrupt flag	Implied	CLI	1	58	N V - B D I Z C 0
CLV Clear overflow flag	Implied	CLV	1	B8	N V - B D I Z C 0
CMP Compare memory and accumulator	Immediate Zero Page Zero Page X Absolute Absolute X Absolute Y (Indirect X) (Indirect) Y	CMP #Oper CMP Oper CMP Oper X CMP Oper CMP Oper X CMP Oper Y CMP (Oper X) CMP (Oper) Y	2 2 2 3 3 3 2 2	C9 C5 D5 CD DD D9 C1 D1	N V - B D I Z C ● ● ●
CPX Compare memory and index X	Immediate Zero Page Absolute	CPX #Oper CPX Oper CPX Oper	2 2 3	E0 E4 EC	N V - B D I Z C ● ● ●
CPY Compare memory and index Y	Immediate Zero Page Absolute	CPY #Oper CPY Oper CPY Oper	2 2 3	C0 C4 CC	N V - B D I Z C ● ● ●
DEC Decrement memory by one	Zero Page Zero Page X Absolute Absolute X	DEC Oper DEC Oper X DEC Oper DEC Oper X	2 2 3 3	C6 D6 CE DE	N V - B D I Z C ● ●
DEX Decrement index X by one	Implied	DEX	1	DA	N V - B D I Z C ● ●
DEY Decrement index Y by one	Implied	DEY	1	88	N V - B D I Z C ● ●

75Ø1 Instruction Codes

Name Description	Addressing Mode	Assembly Language Form	No Bytes	HEX OP Code	Status Register
RTI Return from interrupt	Implied	RTI	1	40	N V - B D I Z C ● ● ● ● ● ● ● ●
RTS Return from subroutine	Implied	RTS	1	60	N V - B D I Z C
SBC Subtract memory from accumulator with borrow	Immediate Zero Page Zero Page X Absolute Absolute.X Absolute.Y (Indirect.X) (Indirect).Y	SBC #Oper SBC Oper SBC Oper X SBC Oper SBC Oper.X SBC Oper Y SBC (Oper X) SBC (Oper) Y	2 2 2 3 3 3 2 2	E9 E5 F5 ED FD F9 E1 F1	N V - B D I Z C ● ● ● ●
SEC Set carry flag	Implied	SEC	1	38	N V - B D I Z C 1
SED Set decimal mode	Implied	SED	1	F8	N V - B D I Z C 1
SEI Set interrupt disable status	Implied	SEI	1	78	N V - B D I Z C 1
STA Store accumulator in memory	Zero Page Zero Page X Absolute Absolute.X Absolute Y (Indirect.X) (Indirect) Y	STA Oper STA Oper.X STA Oper STA Oper X STA Oper Y STA (Oper.X) STA (Oper).Y	2 2 3 3 3 2 2	85 95 8D 9D 99 81 91	N V - B D I Z C
STX Store index X in memory	Zero Page Zero Page Y Absolute	STX Oper STX Oper Y STX Oper	2 2 3	86 96 8E	N V - B D I Z C
STY Store index Y in memory	Zero Page Zero Page X Absolute	STY Oper STY Oper.X STY Oper	2 2 3	84 94 8C	N V - B D I Z C
TAX Transfer accumulator to index X	Implied	TAX	1	AA	N V - B D I Z C ● ●
TAY Transfer accumulator to index Y	Implied	TAY	1	A8	N V - B D I Z C ● ●
TSX Transfer stack pointer to index X	Implied	TSX	1	BA	N V - B D I Z C ● ●

75∅1 Instruction Codes

Name Description	Addressing Mode	Assembly Language Form	No Bytes	HEX OP Code	Status Register
TXA Transfer index X to accumulator	Implied	TXA	1	BA	N V - B D I Z C ● ●
TXS Transfer index X to stack pointer	Implied	TXS	1	9A	N V - B D I Z C
TYA Transfer index Y to accumulator	Implied	TYA	1	98	N V - B D I Z C ● ●

75Ø1 Microprocessor Operation Codes
in numerical value order

00 — BRK	2F — ???	5E — LSR — Sbsolute X
01 — ORA — (Indirect X)	30 — BMI	5F — ???
02 — ???	31 — AND — (Indirect) Y	60 — RTS
03 — ???	32 — ???	61 — ADC — (Indirect X)
04 — ???	33 — ???	62 — ???
05 — ORA — Zero Page	34 — ???	63 — ???
06 — ASL — Zero Page	35 — AND — Zero Page X	64 — ???
07 — ???	36 — ROL —Zero Page X	65 — ACD — Zero Page
08 — PHP	37 — ???	66 — ROR — Zero Page
09 — ORA — Immediate	38 — SEC	67 — ???
0A — ASL — Accumulator	39 — AND — Absolute Y	68 — PLA
0B — ???	3A — ???	69 — ADC — Immediate
0C — ???	3B — ???	6A — ROR — Accumulator
0D — ORA — Absolute	3C — ???	6B — ???
0E — ASL — Absolute	3D — AND — Absolute X	6C — JMP — Indirect
0F — ???	3E — ROL — Absolute X	6D — ADC — Absolute
10 — BPL	3F — NOP	6E — ROR — Absolute
11 — ORA — (Indirect) Y	40 — RTI	6F — ???
12 — ???	41 — EOR — (Indirect X)	70 — BVS
13 — ???	42 — ???	71 — ADC — (Indirect) Y
14 — ???	43 — ???	72 — ???
15 — ORA — Zero Page X	44 — ???	73 — ???
16 — ASL — Zero Page.X	45 — EOR — Zero Page	74 — ???
17 — ???	46 — LSR — Zero Page	75 — ADC — Zero Page X
18 — CLC	47 — ???	76 — ROR — Zero Page X
19 — ORA — Absolute Y	48 — PHA	77 — ???
1A — ???	49 — EOR — Immediate	78 — SEI
1B — ???	4A — LSR — Accumulator	79 — ADC — Absolute Y
1C — ???	4B — ???	7A — ???
1D — ORA — Absolute X	4C — JMP — Absolute	7B — ???
1E — ASL — Absolute X	4D — EOR — Absolute	7C — ???
1F — ???	4E — LSR — Absolute	7D — ADC — Absolute X
20 — JSR	4F — ???	7E — ROR — Absolute X
21 — AND — (Indirect X)	50 — BVC	7F — ???
22 — ???	51 — EOR (Indirect) Y	80 — ???
23 — ???	52 — ???	81 — STA — (Indirect X)
24 — BIT — Zero Page	53 — ???	82 — ???
25 — AND — Zero Page	54 — ???	83 — ???
26 — ROL — Zero Page	55 — EOR — Zero Page X	84 — STY — Zero Page
27 — ???	56 — LSR — Zero Page X	85 — STA — Zero Page
28 — PLP	57 — ???	86 — STX — Zero Page
29 — AND — Immediate	58 — CLI	87 — ???
2A — ROL — Accumulator	59 — EOR — Absolute Y	88 — DEY
2B — ???	5A — ???	89 — ???
2C — BIT — Absolute	5B — ???	8A — TXA
2D — AND — Absolute	5C — ???	8B — ???
2E — ROL — Absolute	5D — EOR — Absolute X	8C — STY — Absolute

8D — STA — Absolute	B4 — LDY — Zero Page.X	DB — ???
8E — STX — Absolute	B5 — LDA — Zero Page.X	DC — ???
8F — ???	B6 — LDX — Zero Page.Y	DD — CMP — Absolute.X
90 — BCC	B7 — ???	DE — DEC — Absolute.X
91 — STA — (Indirect).Y	B8 — CLV	DF —
92 — ???	B9 — LDA — Absolute.Y	E0 — CPX — Immediate
93 — ???	BA — TSX	E1 — SBC — (Indirect.X)
94 — STY — Zero Page.X	BB — ???	E2 — ???
95 — STA — Zero Page.X	BC — LDY — Absolute.X	E3 — ???
96 — STX — Zero Page.Y	BD — LDA — Absolute.X	E4 — CPX — Zero Page
97 — ???	BE — LDX — Absolute.Y	E5 — SBC — Zero Page
98 — TYA	BF — ???	E6 — INC — Zero Page
99 — STA — Absolute.Y	C0 — CPY — Immediate	E7 — ???
9A — TXS	C1 — CMP — (Indirect.X)	E8 — INX
9B — ???	C2 — ???	E9 — SBC — Immediate
9C — ???	C3 — ???	EA — NOP
9D — STA — Absolute.X	C4 — CPY — Zero Page	EB — ???
9E — ???	C5 — CMP — Zero Page	EC — CPX — Absolute
9F — ???	C6 — DEC — Zero Page	ED — SBC — Absolute
A0 — LDY — Immediate	C7 — ???	EE — INC — Absolute
A1 — LDA — (Indirect.X)	C8 — INY	EF — ???
A2 — LDX — Immediate	C9 — CMP — Immediate	F0 — BEQ
A3 — ???	CA — DEX	F1 — SBC — (Indirect).Y
A4 — LDY — Zero Page	CB — ???	F2 — ???
A5 — LDA — Zero Page	CC — CPY — Absolute	F3 — ???
A6 — LDX — Zero Page	CD — CMP — Absolute	F4 — ???
A7 — ???	CE — DEC — Absolute	F5 — SBC — Zero Page.X
A8 — *TAY	CF — ???	F6 — INC — Zero Page.X
A9 — LDA — Immediate	D0 — BNE	F7 — ???
AA — TAX	C1 — CMP — (Indirect).Y	F8 — SED
AB — ???	D2 — ???	F9 — SBC — Absolute.Y
AC — LDY — Absolute	D3 — ???	FA — ???
AD — LDA — Absolute	D4 — ???	FB — ???
AE — LDX — Absolute	D5 — CMP — Zero Page.X	FC — ???
AF — ???	D6 — DEC — Zero Page.X	FD — SBC — Absolute.X
B0 — BCS	D7 — ???	FE — INC — Absolute.X
B1 — LDA — (Indirect).Y	D8 — CLD	FF — ???
B2 — ???	D9 — CMP — Absolute.Y	
B3 — ???	DA — ???	

???Undefined Operation

Appendix 2

75Ø1 Microprocessor Registers

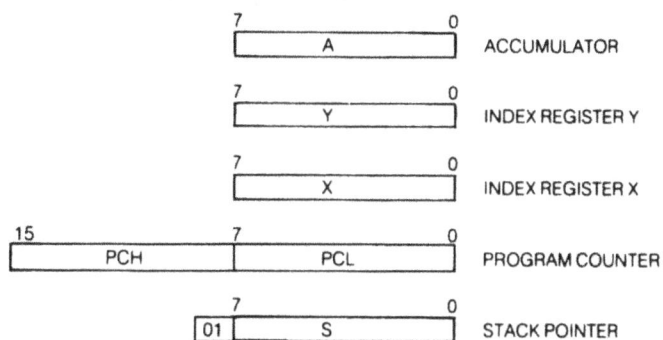

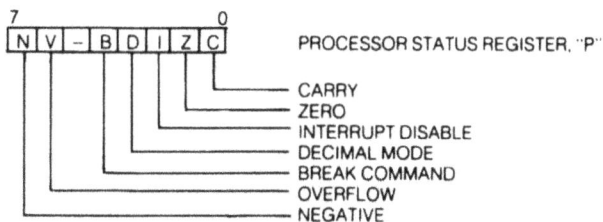

```
  7              0
 [      A       ]    ACCUMULATOR

  7              0
 [      Y       ]    INDEX REGISTER Y

  7              0
 [      X       ]    INDEX REGISTER X

 15          7              0
 [  PCH    ][    PCL     ]   PROGRAM COUNTER

          7              0
    [01][    S      ]    STACK POINTER


  7                    0
 [N|V|–|B|D|I|Z|C]    PROCESSOR STATUS REGISTER, "P"
  │ │   │ │ │ │ └──── CARRY
  │ │   │ │ │ └────── ZERO
  │ │   │ │ └──────── INTERRUPT DISABLE
  │ │   │ └────────── DECIMAL MODE
  │ │   └──────────── BREAK COMMAND
  │ └──────────────── OVERFLOW
  └────────────────── NEGATIVE
```

Hexadecimal to Decimal Conversion Table
Least Significant Digit

HEX	0		1		2		3		4		5		6		7		8		9		A		B		C		D		E		F	
	Low Byte	High Byte	Low Byte	High Byte	Low Byte	High Byte	Low Byte	High Byte	Low Byte	High Byte	Low Byte	High Byte	Low Byte	High Byte	Low Byte	High Byte	Low Byte	High Byte	Low Byte	High Byte	Low Byte	High Byte	Low Byte	High Byte	Low Byte	High Byte	Low Byte	High Byte	Low Byte	High Byte	Low Byte	High Byte
0	0	0	1	256	2	512	3	768	4	1024	5	1280	6	1536	7	1792	8	2048	9	2304	10	2560	11	2816	12	3072	13	3328	14	3584	15	3840
1	16	4096	17	4352	18	4608	19	4864	20	5120	21	5376	22	5632	23	5888	24	6144	25	6400	26	6656	27	6912	28	7168	29	7424	30	7680	31	7936
2	32	8192	33	8448	34	8704	35	8960	36	9216	37	9472	38	9728	39	9984	40	10240	41	10496	42	10752	43	11008	44	11264	45	11520	46	11776	47	12032
3	48	12288	49	12544	50	12800	51	13056	52	13312	53	13568	54	13824	55	14080	56	14336	57	14592	58	14848	59	15104	60	15360	61	15616	62	15872	63	16128
4	64	16384	65	16640	66	16896	67	17152	68	17408	69	17664	70	17920	71	18176	72	18432	73	18688	74	18944	75	19200	76	19456	77	19712	78	19968	79	20224
5	80	20480	81	20736	82	20992	83	21248	84	21504	85	21760	86	22016	87	22272	88	22528	89	22784	90	23040	91	23296	92	23552	93	23808	94	24064	95	24320
6	96	24576	97	24832	98	25088	99	25344	100	25600	101	25856	102	26112	103	26368	104	26624	105	26880	106	27136	107	27392	108	27648	109	27904	110	28160	111	28416
7	112	28672	113	28928	114	29184	115	29440	116	29696	117	29952	118	30208	119	30464	120	30720	121	30976	122	31232	123	31488	124	31744	125	32000	126	32256	127	32512
8	128	32768	129	33024	130	33280	131	33536	132	33792	133	34048	134	34304	135	34560	136	34816	137	35072	138	35328	139	35584	140	35840	141	36096	142	36352	143	36608
9	144	36864	145	37120	146	37376	147	37632	148	37888	149	38144	150	38400	151	38656	152	38912	153	39168	154	39424	155	39680	156	39936	157	40192	158	40448	159	40704
A	160	40960	161	41216	162	41472	163	41728	164	41984	165	42240	166	42496	167	42752	168	43008	169	43264	170	43520	171	43776	172	44032	173	44288	174	44544	175	44800
B	176	45056	177	45312	178	45568	179	45824	180	46080	181	46336	182	46592	183	46848	184	47104	185	47360	186	47616	187	47872	188	48128	189	48384	190	48640	191	48896
C	192	49152	193	49408	194	49664	195	49920	196	50176	197	50432	198	50688	199	50944	200	51200	201	51456	202	51712	203	51968	204	52224	205	52480	206	52736	207	52992
D	208	53248	209	53504	210	53760	211	54016	212	54272	213	54528	214	54784	215	55040	216	55296	217	55552	218	55808	219	56064	220	56320	221	56576	222	56832	223	57088
E	224	57344	225	57600	226	57856	227	58112	228	58368	229	58624	230	58880	231	59136	232	59392	233	59648	234	59904	235	60160	236	60416	237	60672	238	60928	239	61184
F	240	61440	241	61696	242	61952	243	62208	244	62464	245	62720	246	62976	247	63232	248	63488	249	63744	250	64000	251	64256	252	64512	253	64768	254	65024	255	65280

Most Significant Digit

Appendix 3

Hexadecimal to Decimal Conversion Table

This table can be used to convert up to four digit hex numbers to decimal.

How to use the table:

1. Divide the number into groups of two digits,
   e.g. $F17B \rightarrow$ F1   7B
   $2A   \rightarrow$ 2A

2. Take the low byte of the number (from above 7B or 2A) and look it up in the chart. Find the most significant digit (7) in the column on the left, find the least significant digit (8) in the row along the top, and find the box in which the row (7) and the column (B) cross. In that box you will find 2 numbers,   123 31488   . These are the values of 7B in the low byte and the high byte. Since we are looking up the low byte, take the value 123. Now find the location of the high byte of our number (F1) on the chart. The box here contains   241 61696   . Since we are now dealing with the high byte, take the value 61696 from that box and add it to the value we found earlier for the low byte 123.

   61696
   + 123
   ―――――
   61819   which is the decimal value of $F17B
   ―――――

NOTE: to find the decimal value of a two digit number, e.g. 2A, look it up in the chart taking the low byte value (42). For a one digit number, e.g. E, create a two digit number by adding a leading zero (ØE), and similarly make three digit numbers four digits with a leading zero.

Appendix 4

Relative Branch and Two's Complement Numbering Tables

1. To calculate relative branches, locate the address immediately after the location of the branch instruction. Count the number of bytes from there to where you want the branch to end up. If the destination is before the first byte, use the backward branch table and if not, use the forward branch table. Look up the displacement (the number you counted) in the body of the appropriate chart and read off the high and low digits of the branch from the sides. This can also be used in reverse, by looking up a branch on the sides to find the displacement taken in the body of the chart.

2. To convert from a signed decimal number between −128 and 127 to a hex two's complement number, find your decimal number in the body of the appropriate chart (positives and negatives) and read off the hex two's complement number from the sides (high digit, low digit). The reverse process (two's complement hex to signed decimal) is simply a matter of finding the high digit on the column on the left, the low digit on the top row, reading off the number where the row and column meet, and if in the negative chart make the number negative.

Relative Branch Tables and
Two's Complement Numbering tables

FORWARD RELATIVE BRANCH   POSITIVE NUMBERS

low\hi	0	1	2	3	4	5	6	7	8	9	A	B	C	D	E	F
0	0	1	2	3	4	5	6	7	8	9	10	11	12	13	14	15
1	16	17	18	19	20	21	22	23	24	25	26	27	28	29	30	31
2	32	33	34	35	36	37	38	39	40	41	42	43	44	45	46	47
3	48	49	50	51	52	53	54	55	56	57	58	59	60	61	62	63
4	64	65	66	67	68	69	70	71	72	73	74	75	76	77	78	79
5	80	81	82	83	84	85	86	87	88	89	90	91	92	93	94	95
6	96	97	98	99	100	101	102	103	104	105	106	107	108	109	110	111
7	112	113	114	115	116	117	118	119	120	121	122	123	124	125	126	127

BACKWARD RELATIVE BRANCH   NEGATIVE NUMBERS

low\hi	0	1	2	3	4	5	6	7	8	9	A	B	C	D	E	F
8	128	127	126	125	124	123	122	121	120	119	118	117	116	115	114	113
9	112	111	110	109	108	107	106	105	104	103	102	101	100	99	98	97
A	96	95	94	93	92	91	90	89	88	87	86	85	84	83	82	81
B	80	79	78	77	76	75	74	73	72	71	70	69	68	67	66	65
C	64	63	62	61	60	59	58	57	56	55	54	53	52	51	50	49
D	48	47	46	45	44	43	42	41	40	39	38	37	36	35	34	33
E	32	31	30	29	28	27	26	25	24	23	22	21	20	19	18	17
F	16	15	14	13	12	11	10	9	8	7	6	5	4	3	2	1

Label	Address	Description
USER	$00EA-00EB	Screen editor color IP
KEYTAB	$00EC-00ED	Key scan table indirect
TMPKEY	$00EE	
NDX	$00EF	Index to keyboard queue
STPFLG	$00F0	Pause flag
TO	$00F1-00F2	Monitor zero-page storage
CHRPTR	$00F3	
BUFEND	$00F4	
CHKSUM	$00F5	Temp for checksum calculation
LENGTH	$00F6	
PASS	$00F7	Which pass we are doing
TYPE	$00F8	Type of block
USEKDY	$00F9	Bit 7=1 for Write; Bit 6=1 for Read
XSTOP	$00FA	Save xreq for quick stopkey test
CURBNK	$00FB	Current bank configuration
XON	$00FC	Char to send for a x-on
XOFF	$00FD	Char to send for a x-off
SEDT2	$00FE	Editor temporary use
LOFBUF	$00FF	
FBUFFR	$0100-010F	Temp locations for:
SAVEA	$0110	Save
SAVEX	$0111	Restore
SAVEY	$0112	
COLKEY	$0113-0122	Color/luminance table in RAM
SYSSTK	$0124-01FF	System Stack
BUF	$0200-0258	BASIC / Monitor buffer
OLDLIN	$0259-025A	BASIC storage
OLDTXT	$025B-025C	BASIC storage
	$025D-02AC	BASIC/DOS interface area

100

Appendix 5

Detailed Memory Map of the C-16

Label	Address Hex	Decimal	Description
PDIR	$0000	0	7501 on-chip data direction register
PORT	$0001	1	7501 on-chip 8-bit Input/Output register
SRCHTK	$0002	2	Token value of search (run-time stack)
ZPVEC1	$0003-0004	3-4	Temp (renumber)
ZPVEC2	$0005-0006	5-6	Temp (renumber)
CHARAC	$0007	7	Search character
ENDCHR	$0008	8	Flag: scan for quote at end of string
TRMPOS	$0009	9	Screen column from last TAB
VERCK	$000A	10	Flag: 0 = Load, 1 = Verify
COUNT	$000B	11	Input Buffer pointer/ No. of subscripts
DIMFLG	$000C	12	Flag: Default array DIMension
VALTYP	$000D	13	Data type: $FF = String, $00 = Numeric
INTFLG	$000E	14	Data type: $80 = integer, $00 = Floating
DORES	$000F	15	Flag: DATA scan/LIST quote/garbage coll.
SUBFLG	$0010	16	Flag: Subscript ref/user function call
INPFLG	$0011	17	Flag: $00 = Input, $40 = GET, $98 = READ
TANSGN	$0012	18	Flag: TAN sign/ comparison result
CHANNL	$0013	19	Flag: Input prompt
LINNUM	$0014-0015	20-21	Temp: Integer value
TEMPPT	$0016	22	Pointer: temporary string stack
LASTPT	$0017-0018	23-24	Last tempstring address
TEMPST	$0019-0021	25-33	Stack for temporary strings
INDEX1	$0022-0023	34-35	Utility Pointer area
INDEX2	$0024-0025	36-37	Utility Pointer area
RESHO	$0026	38	
RESMOH	$0027	39	
RESMO	$0028	40	

RESLO	$0029	41	
	$002A	42	
TXTTAB	$002B-002C	43-44	Pointer: Start of BASIC Text
VARTAB	$002D-002E	45-46	Pointer: Start of BASIC Variables
ARYTAB	$002F-0030	47-48	Pointer: Start of BASIC Arrays
STREND	$0031-0032	49-50	Pointer: End of BASIC Arrays (+1)
FRETOP	$0033-0034	51-52	Pointer: Bottom of string storage
FRESPC	$0035-0036	53-54	Utility string Pointer
MEMSIZ	$0037-0038	55-56	Pointer: Highest address used by BASIC
CURLIN	$0039-003A	57-58	Current BASIC line number
TXTPTR	$003B-003C	59-60	Previous BASIC line number
FNDPNT	$003D-003E	61-62	
DATLIN	$003F-0040	63-64	Current DATA line number
DATPTR	$0041-0042	65-66	Pointer: Current DATA item address
INPFTR	$0043-0044	67-68	Vector: INPUT routine
VARNAM	$0045-0046	69-70	Current BASIC Variable Name
VARPNT	$0047-0048	71-72	Pointer: Current BASIC Variable data
FORPNT	$0049-004A	73-74	Pointer: Index variable for FOR/NEXT
OPPTR	$004B-004C	75-76	
OPMASK	$004D	77	
DEFPNT	$004E-004F	78-79	
DSCPNT	$0050-0051	80-81	
	$0052	82	
HELPER	$0053	83	
JMPER	$0054	84	
SIZE	$0055	85	
OLDOV	$0056	86	
TEMPF1	$0057	87	
HIGHDS	$0058-0059	88-89	
HIGHTR	$005A-005B	90-91	
	$005C	92	
LOWDS	$005D-005E	93-94	

Label	Address	Dec	Description
LOWTR	$005F	95	
EXPSGN	$0060	96	
FACEXP	$0061	97	Floating-point accumulator #1: exponent
FACHO	$0062	98	Floating-point accumulator #1: mantissa
FACMOH	$0063	99	
FACMO	$0064	100	
FACLO	$0065	101	
FACSGN	$0066	102	Floating-point accumulator #1: sign
SGNFLG	$0067	103	Pointer: series evaluation constant
BITS	$0068	104	Floating-point accumulator #1: Overflow
ARGEXP	$0069	105	Floating-point accumulator #2: Exponent
ARGHO	$006A	106	Floating-point accumulator #2: Mantissa
ARGMOH	$006B	107	
ARGMO	$006C	108	
ARGLO	$006D	109	
ARGSGN	$006E	110	Floating-point accumulator #2: sign
ARISGN	$006F	111	Sign comparison result: accum. #1 vs #2
FACOV	$0070	112	Floating accum. #1: low-order (rounded)
FBUFPT	$0071-0072	113-114	Pointer: Cassette Buffer
AUTINC	$0073-0074	115-116	Line increment value for auto (0 = off)
MVDFLG	$0075	117	Flag if 10K hi-res allocated
KEYNUM	$0076	118	
KEYSIZ	$0077	119	
SYNTMF	$0078	120	Used as temp for indirect loads
DSDESC	$0079-007B	121-123	Descriptor for ds$
TOS	$007C-007D	124-125	Top of run-time stack
TMPTON	$007E-007F	126-127	Temps used by music (tone & volume)
VOICNO	$0080	128	
RUNMOD	$0081	129	
POINT	$0082	130	
GRAPHM	$0083	131	Current graphic mode
COLSEL	$0084	132	Current color selected

Label	Address	Decimal	Description
MC1	$0085	133	Multicolor one
FGC	$0086	134	Foreground color
SCXMAX	$0087	135	Maximum # of columns
SCYMAX	$0088	136	Maximum # of rows
LTFLAG	$0089	137	Paint-left Flag
RTFLAG	$008A	138	Paint-right Flag
STOPNE	$008B	139	Stop paint if not Background color
GRAPNT	$008C-008D	140-141	
VTEMP1	$008E	142	
VTEMP2	$008F	143	
STATUS	$0090	144	Kernal I/O status word: ST
STKEY	$0091	145	Flag: STOP key / RVS key
SPVERR	$0092	146	Temp
VERFCK	$0093	147	Flag: 0 = load, 1 = verify
C3P0	$0094	148	Flag: serial bus - output char buffered
BFOUR	$0095	149	Buffered character for serial bus
XSAV	$0096	150	Temp for basin
LDTND	$0097	151	# of open files / index to file table
DFLTN	$0098	152	Default input device (0)
DFLTO	$0099	153	Default output (CMD) device (3)
MSGFLG	$009A	154	Flag: $80 = direct mode. $00 = program
SAL	$009B	155	Tape pass 1 error log
SAH	$009C	156	Tape pass 2 error log
EAL	$009D	157	
EAH	$009E	158	
T1	$009F-00A0	159-160	Temp data area
T2	$00A1-00A2	161-162	Temp data area
TIME	$00A3-00A5	163-165	Real-time jiffy clock (approx) 1/60 sec
R2D2	$00A6	166	Serial bus usage
TPBYTE	$00A7	167	Byte to be written/read on/off tape
BSOUR1	$00A8	168	Temp used by serial routine
FPVERR	$00A9	169	

Label	Address	Description
DCOUNT	$00AA	Length of current filename
FNLEN	$00AB	Current logical file number
LA	$00AC	Current secondary address
SA	$00AD	Current device number
FA	$00AE	Pointer: Current file name
FILDR	$00AF-00B0	
ERRSUM	$00B1	
STAL	$00B2	I/O start address: low byte
STAH	$00B3	I/O start address: high byte
MEMUSS	$00B4-00B5	Load RAM base
TAFEBS	$00B6-00B7	Base pointer to cassette base
TMP2	$00B8-00B9	
WRBASE	$00BA-00BB	Pointer to data for tape writes
IMPARM	$00BC-00BD	Pointer to immediate string for primms
FETPTR	$00BE-00BF	Pointer to be fetched in bank fetch
SEDSAL	$00C0-00C1	Temp for scrolling
RVS	$00C2	RVS field flag on
INDX	$00C3	
LSXP	$00C4	X position at start
LSTP	$00C5	
SFDX	$00C6	Flag: shift mode for print
CRSW	$00C7	Flag: INPUT or GET from keyboard
PNT	$00C8-00C9	Pointer: Current screen line address
PNTR	$00CA	Cursor column on current line
QTSW	$00CB	Flag: Editor in quote mode, $00 = no
SEDT1	$00CC	Editor temp in use
TBLX	$00CD	Current cursor physical line number
DATAX	$00CE	Temp data area
INSRT	$00CF	Flag: Insert mode, > 0 = # INST's
	$00D0-$00D7	Area for use by speech software
	$00D8-00E8	Area for use by application software
CIRSEG	$00E9	Screen line link table/editor temps

105

Label	Address	Decimal	Description
XCNT	$025D	605	DOS loop counter
FNBUFR	$025E-026D	606-621	String storage for filename
DOSF1L	$026E	622	DOS filename 1 length
DOSDS1	$026F	623	DOS disk drive 1
DOSF1A	$0270-0271	624-625	DOS filename 1 address
DOSF2L	$0272	626	DOS filename 2 length
DOSDS2	$0273	627	DOS disk drive 2
DOSF2A	$0274-0275	628-629	DOS filename 2 address
DOSLA	$0276	630	DOS logical address
DOSFA	$0277	631	DOS physical address
DOSSA	$0278	632	DOS secondary address
DOSDID	$0279-027A	633-634	DOS disk identifier
DIDCHK	$027B	635	DOS DID flag
DOSSTR	$027C	636	DOS output string buffer
DOSSPC	$027D-02AC	637-684	Area used to build DOS string

Area used by Graphics Routines

Label	Address	Decimal	Description
XPOS	$02AD-02AE	685-686	Current x position
YPOS	$02AF-02B0	687-688	Current y position
XDEST	$02B1-02B2	689-690	X coordinate destination
YDEST	$02B3-02B4	691-692	Y coordinate destination
XABS	$02B5-02B6	693-694	
YABS	$02B7-02B8	695-696	
XSGN	$02B9-02BA	697-698	
YSGN	$02BB-02BC	699-700	
FCT1	$02BD-02BE	701-702	
FCT2	$02BF-02C0	703-704	
ERRVAL	$02C1-02C2	705-706	
LESSER	$02C3	707	
GREATR	$02C4	708	
ANGSGN	$02C5	709	Sign of angle

SINVAL	$02C6-02C7	710-711	Sine of value of angle
COSVAL	$02C8-02C9	712-713	Cosine of value of angle
ANGCNT	$02CA-02CB	714-715	Temp storage for angle/distance routines

Start of multiply defined area #1

BNR	$02CC	716	Placeholder
ENR	$02CD	717	Pointer to begin no.
	$02CE	718	Pointer to end no.
DOLR	$02CF	719	Dollar flag
FLAG	$02D0	720	Comma flag
SWE	$02D1	721	Counter
USGN	$02D2	722	Sign exponent
UEXP	$02D3	723	Pointer to exponent
VN	$02D4	724	# of digits before decimal point
CHSN	$02D5	725	Justify flag
VF	$02D6	726	# of sig figs before decimal point
NF	$02D7	727	# of sig figs after decimal point
POSP	$02D8	728	+/- flag (field)
FESP	$02D9	729	Exponent flag (field)
ETOF	$02DA	730	Switch
CFORM	$02DB	731	Char counter (field)
SNO	$02DC	732	Sign number
BLFD	$02DD	733	Blank/star field
BEGFD	$02DE	734	Pointer to beginning of field
LFOR	$02DF	735	Length of format
ENDFD	$02E0	736	Pointer to end of field

Start of multiply defined area #2

| XCENTR | $02CC-02CD | 716-717 | |
| YCENTR | $02CE-02CF | 718-719 | |

XDIST1	$02D0-02D1	720-721	
YDIST1	$02D2-02D3	722-723	
XDIST2	$02D4-02D5	724-725	
YDIST2	$02D6-02D7	726-727	
	$02D8-02D9	728-729	Placeholder
COLCNT	$02DA	730	Character column counter
ROWCNT	$02DB	731	Character row counter
STRCNT	$02DC	732	

Start of multiply defined area #3

XCORD1	$02CC-02CD	716-717	
YCORD1	$02CE-02CF	718-719	
BOXANG	$02D0-02D1	720-721	Rotation angle
XCOUNT	$02D2-02D3	722-723	
YCOUNT	$02D4-02D5	724-725	
BXLENG	$02D6-02D7	726-727	Length of a side
XCORD2	$02D8-02D9	728-729	
YCORD2	$02DA-02DB	730-731	
XCIRCL	$02CC-02CD	716-717	Circle center, X coordinate
YCIRCL	$02CE-02CF	718-719	Circle center, Y coordinate
XRADUS	$02D0-02D1	720-721	X radius
YRADUS	$02D2-02D3	722-723	Y radius
ROTANG	$02D4-02D5	724-725	Rotation angle
ANGBEG	$02D8-02D9	728-729	Arc angle start
ANGEND	$02DA-02DB	730-731	Arc angle end
XRCOS	$02DC-02DD	732-733	X radius * cos (rotation angle)
YRSIN	$02DE-02DF	734-735	Y radius * sin (rotation angle)
XRSIN	$02E0-02E1	736-737	X radius * sin (rotation angle)
YRCOS	$02E2-02E3	738-739	Y radius * cos (rotation angle)

Start of multiply defined area #4

Label	Address	Decimal	Description
	$02CC	716	Placeholder
KEYLEN	$02CD	717	
KEYNXT	$02CE	718	
STRSZ	$02CF	719	String length
GETTYP	$02D0	720	Replace string mode
STRPTR	$02D1	721	String position counter
OLDBYT	$02D2	722	Old bit map byte
NEWBYT	$02D3	723	New string or bit map byte
	$02D4	724	Placeholder
XSIZE	$02D5-02D6	725-726	Shape column length
YSIZE	$02D7-02D8	727-728	Shape row length
XSAVE	$02D9-02DA	729-730	Temp for column length
STRADR	$02DB-02DC	731-732	Save shape string descriptor
BITIDX	$02DD	733	Bit index into byte
SAVSIZ	$02DE-02E1	734-737	Temporary working storage
CHRFAG	$02E4	740	High byte address of character ROM for character definitions.
BITCNT	$02E5	741	Temp for GSHAPE
SCALEM	$02E6	742	Scale mode flag
WIDTH	$02E7	743	Double width flag
FILFLG	$02E8	744	Box fill flag
BITMSK	$02E9	745	Temp for bit mask
NUMCNT	$02EA	746	
TRCFLG	$02EB	747	Flags trace mode
T3	$02EC	748	
T4	$02ED-02EE	749-750	
VTEMP3	$02EF	751	Graphics temp storage
VTEMP4	$02F0	752	
VTEMP5	$02F1	753	
ADRAY1	$02F2-02F3	754-755	Vector: convert floating to integer
ADRAY2	$02F4-02F5	756-757	Vector: convert integer to floating

Label	Address	Decimal	Description
BNKVEC	$02F6-02FD	758-765	Vector for function cartridge users
IERROR	$02FE-02FF	766-767	Indirect Error (output error in X)
IMAIN	$0300-0301	768-769	Indirect Main (system direct loop)
ICRNCH	$0302-0303	770-771	Indirect Crunch (tokenisation routine)
IQPLOP	$0304-0305	772-773	Indirect List (Character list)
IGONE	$0306-0307	774-775	Indirect Gone (Character dispatch)
IEVAL	$0308-0309	776-777	Indirect Eval (symbol evaluation)
IESCLK	$030A-030B	778-779	Escape token crunch
IESCPR	$030C-030D	780-781	
IESCEX	$030E-030F	782-783	
ITIME	$0310-0311	784-785	
	$0312-0313	786-787	
CINV	$0314-0315	788-789	IRQ RAM Vector
CBINV	$0316-0317	790-791	BRK instruction RAM Vector
IOPEN	$0318-0319	792-793	Indirect Vectors for code
ICLOSE	$031A-031B	794-795	
ICHKIN	$031C-031D	796-797	
ICKOUT	$031E-031F	798-799	
ICLRCH	$0320-0321	800-801	
IBASIN	$0322-0323	802-803	
IBSOUT	$0324-0325	804-805	
ISTOP	$0326-0327	806-807	
IGETIN	$0328-0329	808-809	
ICLALL	$032A-032B	810-811	
USRCMD	$032C-032D	812-813	
ILOAD	$032E-032F	814-815	
ISAVE	$0330-0331	816-817	Save stack pointer
	$0332	818	
TAFBUF	$0333-03F2	819-1010	Cassette tape buffer
WRLEN	$03F3-03F4	1011-1012	Length of data to be written to tape
RDCNT	$03F5-03F6	1013-1014	Length of data to be read from tape

Label	Address	Decimal	Description
INFQUE	$03F7-0436	1015-1078	RS-232 input queue
ESTAKL	$0437-0454	1079-1108	
ESTAKH	$0455-0472	1109-1138	
CHRGET	$0473-0478	1139-1144	
CHRGOT	$0479-0484	1145-1156	
QNUM	$0485-0493	1157-1171	
INDSUB	$0494-04A1	1172-1185	Shared ROM fetch subroutine
ZERO	$04A2-04A4	1186-1188	Numeric constant for BASIC
INDTXT	$04A5-04AF	1189-1199	Text pointer
INDIN1	$04B0-04BA	1200-1210	Index % Index 1
INDIN2	$04BB-04C5	1211-1221	Index 2
INDST1	$04C6-04D0	1222-1232	String 1
INDLOW	$04D1-04DB	1233-1243	
INDFMO	$04DC-04E6	1244-1254	
PUFILL	$04E7	1255	Print using fill symbol
PUCOMA	$04E8	1256	Print using comma symbol
PUDOT	$04E9	1257	Print using period symbol
PUMONY	$04EA	1258	Print using dollar sign
TMPDES	$04EB-04EE	1259-1262	Temp forinstr
ERRNUM	$04EF	1263	Last error number
ERRLIN	$04F0-04F1	1264-1265	Line number of last error
TRAPNO	$04F2-04F3	1266-1267	Line to go to on error
TMPTRP	$04F4	1268	Temp: hold trap number
ERRTXT	$04F5-04F6	1269-1270	
OLDSTK	$04F7	1271	
TMPTXT	$04F8-04F9	1272-1273	
TMPLIN	$04FA-04FB	1274-1275	
MTIMLO	$04FC-04FD	1276-1277	Table of pending jiffies in 2's comp.
MTIMHI	$04FE-04FF	1278-1279	
USRPOK	$0500-0502	1280-1282	
RNDX	$0503-0507	1283-1287	
DEJAVU	$0508	1288	'cold' or 'warm' start status

Label	Address	Description
LAT	$0509-0512	Logical file numbers
FAT	$0513-051C	Primary device numbers
SAT	$051D-0526	Secondary address
KEYD	$0527-0530	IRQ Keyboard buffer
MEMSTR	$0531-0532	Start of memory
MSIZ	$0533-0534	Top of memory
TIMOUT	$0535	IEEE timout flag
FILEND	$0536	File end flag; 1 = reached, 0 = otherwise
CTALLY	$0537	Number of chars left in buffer (R/W)
CBUFVA	$0538	Number of total valid chars in buffer (R)
TPTR	$0539	Pointer: next char in buffer (R/W)
FLTYPE	$053A	Contains current type of cassette file
COLOR	$053B	Active attribute byte
FLASH	$053C	Character flash flag
	$053D	FREE!!!
HIBASE	$053E	Base location of screen top
XMZX	$053F	
RPTFLG	$0540	Key repeatflag
KOUNT	$0541	
DELAY	$0542	
SHFLAG	$0543	Shift flagbyte
LSTSHF	$0544	Last shift pattern
KEYLOG	$0545-0546	Indirect for keyboard table setup
MODE	$0547	
AUTODN	$0548	Auto scroll down flag 0 = on, >0 = off
LINTMP	$0549	
ROLFLG	$054A	
FORMAT	$054B	Monitor non zero-page storage
	$054C-054E	
WRAP	$054F	
TMPC	$0550	
DIFF	$0551	

Label	Address	Decimal	Description
PCH	$0552	1362	
PCL	$0553	1363	
FLGS	$0554	1364	
ACC	$0555	1365	
XR	$0556	1366	
YR	$0557	1367	
SP	$0558	1368	
INVL	$0559	1369	
INVH	$055A	1370	
CMPFLG	$055B	1371	Used by various monitor routines
BAD	$055C	1372	
KEYIDX	$055D	1373	Used for programmable keys
KEYIDX	$055E	1374	
KEYBUF	$055F-0566	1375-1382	Table for P.F. lengths
PKYBUF	$0567-05E6	1383-1510	P.F. key storage area
KDATA	$05E7	1511	Temp for data write to kennedy
KDYCMD	$05E8	1512	Select for kennedy read or write
KDYNUM	$05E9	1513	Kennedy's device number
KDYPRS	$05EA	1514	Flag: $FF = Kennedy present, $00 = not
KDYTYP	$05EB	1515	Temp for type of open for kennedy
SAVRAM	$05EC-06EB	1516-1771	One whole page used by banking routines
PAT	$05EC-05EF	1516-1519	Physical address table
LNGJMP	$05F0-05F1	1520-1521	Long jump address
FETARG	$05F2	1522	Long jump accumulator
FETXRG	$05F3	1523	Long jump X register
FETSRG	$05F4	1524	Long jump status register
AREAS	$05F5-065D	1525-1629	RAM areas for banking
ASPECH	$065E-06EB	1630-1771	RAM area for speech
STKTOP	$06EC-07AF	1772-1967	BASIC run-time stack
WROUT	$07B0	1968	Byte to be written on tape

Label	Address	Description
PARITY	$07B1	Temp for parity calculations
TT1	$07B2	Temp for write header
TT2	$07B3	Temp for write header
	$07B4	
RDBITS	$07B5	Local index for READBYTE routine
ERRSP	$07B6	Pointer into the error stack
FPERRS	$07B7	Number of first pass errors
DSAMP1	$07B8-07B9	Time constant
DSAMP2	$07BA-07BB	Time constant
ZCELL	$07BC-07BD	Time constant
SRECOV	$07BE	Stack marker for stopkey recover
DRECOV	$07BF	Stack marker for dropkey recover
TRSAVE	$07C0-07C3	Parameters passed to RDBLOK
RDSTMP	$07C4	Temp status save for RDBLOK
LDRSCN	$07C5	# consecutive shorts to find in leader
CDERRM	$07C6	# errors fatal in RD countdown
VSAVE	$07C7	Temp for verify command
T1PIFE	$07C8-07CB	Pipe temp for T1
ENEXT	$07CC	Read error propagate

RS-232 Section

Label	Address	Description
UOUTQ	$07CD	User character to send
UOUTFG	$07CE	Flag: 0 = buffer empty, 1 = full
SOUTQ	$07CF	System character to send
SOUNFG	$07D0	Flag: 0 = buffer empty, 1 = full
INQFPT	$07D1	Pointer: front of input queue
INQRPT	$07D2	Pointer: rear of input queue
INQCNT	$07D3	Number of characters in input queue
ASTAT	$07D4	Temp status for ACIA
AINTMP	$07D5	Temp for input routine
ALSTOP	$07D6	Flag for local pause
ARSTOP	$07D7	Flag for remote pause

APRES	$07D8	Flag: 0 = no ACIA, 1 = ACIA
KLUDES	$07D9-07E4	Indirect routine downloaded
SCBOT	$07E5	
SCTOP	$07E6	
SCLF	$07E7	
SCRT	$07E8	
SCRDIS	$07E9	
INSFLG	$07EA	
LSTCHR	$07EB	
LOGSCR	$07EC	
TCOLOR	$07ED	
BITABL	$07EE-07F1	

Temp Storage for Registers during SYS command:

SAREG	$07F2	Accumulator
SXREG	$07F3	X index register
SYREG	$07F4	Y index register
SPREG	$07F5	Program Counter
LSTX	$07F6	Key scan index
STPDSB	$07F7	Flag to disable CONTROL-S pause
RAMROM	$07F8	MSB for monitor fetches from 0=ROM,1=RAM
COLSW	$07F9	MSB for color/lum table: 0=RAM,1=ROM
FFRMSK	$07FA	ROM mask for split screen
VMBMSK	$07FB	VM base mask for split screen
LSEM	$07FC	Motor lock semaphore for cassette
FALCNT	$07FD	FAL
	$07FE-07FF	
TEDATR	$0800-0BFF	Screen color attribute bytes
TEDSCN	$0C00-0FFF	Screen character pointers
BASBGN	$1000-	Start of BASIC text area
GRBASE	$2000-	Start of BASIC when Hi-res on

```
BMLUM    $1800-1BFF   6144-7167   Luminance table for bit-map screen
BMCOLOR  $1C00-1FFF   7168-8191   Color table for bit-map screen

CHRBAS   $D000-D7FF  53248-       Beginning of 2K character ROM
         $D800-FCFF               KERNAL ROM

         Banking Jump Table

         $FCF1   64753   JMP to Cartridge IRQ routine
         $FCF4   64756   JMP to PHOENIX routine
         $FCF7   64759   JMP to LONG FETCH routine
         $FCFA   64762   JMP to LONG JUMP routine
         $FCFD   64765   JMP to LONG IRQ routine

         Unofficial Jump table

         $FF49   65353   JMP to define function key routine
         $FF4C   65356   JMP to PRINT routine
         $FF4F   65359   JMP to PRIMM routine
         $FF52   65362   JMP to ENTRY routine
         $FF80   65408   Release number of KERNAL  (msb 0=NTSC;1=PAL)

         KERNAL JUMP TABLE

CINT     $FFB1   65409   Initialise screen editor
IOINIT   $FFB4   65412   Initialise I/O devices
RAMTAS   $FFB7   65415   RAM test
RESTOR   $FFBA   65418   Restore vectors to initial values
VECTOR   $FFBD   65421   Change vectors for user
SETMSG   $FF90   65424   Control operating system messages
SECND    $FF93   65427   Send SA after LISTEN
TKSA     $FF96   65430   Send SA after TALK
```

Name	Hex	Decimal	Description
MEMTOP	$FF99	65433	Set/Read top of memory
MEMBOT	$FF9C	65436	Set/Read bottom of memory
SCNKEY	$FF9F	65439	Scan keyboard
SETTMO	$FFA2	65442	Set timeout in DMA disk
ACPTR	$FFA5	65445	Handshake serial bus or DMA disk byte in
CIOUT	$FFA8	65448	Handshake serial bus orDMA disk byte out
UNTLK	$FFAB	65451	Send UNTALK out serial bus or DMA disk
UNLSN	$FFAE	65454	Send UNLISTEN out serial bus or DMA disk
LISTN	$FFB1	65457	Send LISTEN out serial bus or DMA disk
TALK	$FFB4	65460	Send TALK out serial bus or DMA disk
READSS	$FFB7	65463	Return I/O STATUS byte
SETLFS	$FFBA	65466	Set logical file parameters: LA, FA, SA
SETNAM	$FFBD	65469	Set filename length and FN address
OPEN	$FFC0	65472	Open logical file
CLOSE	$FFC3	65475	Close logical file
CHKIN	$FFC6	65478	Open channel in
CHOUT	$FFC9	65481	Open channel out
CLRCH	$FFCC	65484	Close I/O channels
BASIN	$FFCF	65487	Input from channel
BSOUT	$FFD2	65490	Output to channel
LOADSP	$FFD5	65493	Load from file
SAVESP	$FFD8	65496	Save to file
SETTIM	$FFDB	65499	Set internal clock
RDTIM	$FFDE	65502	Read internal clock
STOP	$FFE1	65505	Scan STOP key
GETIN	$FFE4	65508	Get character from queue
CLALL	$FFE7	65511	Close all files
UDTIM	$FFEA	65514	Increment clock
SCRORG	$FFED	65517	Screen organistaion
PLOT	$FFF0	65520	Read/Set X,Y coordinates of cursor
IOBASE	$FFF3	65523	Return location of start of I/O

Appendix 6

The Ted Chip Register Map

Hex	Req	DB7	DB6	DB5	DB4	DB3	DB2	DB1	DB0
$FF00	0	Timer 1 Bit 7	Timer 1 Bit 6	Timer 1 Bit 5	Timer 1 Bit 4	Timer 1 Bit 3	Timer 1 Bit 2	Timer 1 Bit 1	Timer 1 Bit 0
$FF01	1	Timer 1 Bit 15	Timer 1 Bit 14	Timer 1 Bit 13	Timer 1 Bit 12	Timer 1 Bit 11	Timer 1 Bit 10	Timer 1 Bit 9	Timer 1 Bit 8
$FF02	2	Timer 2 Bit 7	Timer 2 Bit 6	Timer 2 Bit 5	Timer 2 Bit 4	Timer 2 Bit 3	Timer 2 Bit 2	Timer 2 Bit 1	Timer 2 Bit 0
$FF03	3	Timer 2 Bit 15	Timer 2 Bit 14	Timer 2 Bit 13	Timer 2 Bit 12	Timer 2 Bit 11	Timer 2 Bit 10	Timer 2 Bit 9	Timer 2 Bit 8
$FF04	4	Timer 3 Bit 7	Timer 3 Bit 6	Timer 3 Bit 5	Timer 3 Bit 4	Timer 3 Bit 3	Timer 3 Bit 2	Timer 3 Bit 1	Timer 3 Bit 0
$FF05	5	Timer 3 Bit 15	Timer 3 Bit 14	Timer 3 Bit 13	Timer 3 Bit 12	Timer 3 Bit 11	Timer 3 Bit 10	Timer 3 Bit 9	Timer 3 Bit 8
$FF06	6	test	Extend color	Bit map mode	blank	24/25 row	Vert. Scroll2	Vert. Scroll1	Vert. Scroll0
$FF07	7	Reverse off	PAL/ NTSC	freeze	Multi color	39/40 col	Horz. Scroll2	Horz. Scroll1	Horz. Scroll0
$FF08	8	K E Y B O A R D L A T C H							
$FF09	9	Request Intrupt	Timer3 Intrupt	N/C	Timer2 Intrupt	Timer1 Intrupt	Lt.pen Intrupt	Raster Intrupt	N/C
$FF0A	10	N/C	Enable T3.Int	N/C	Enable T2.Int	Enable T1.Int	Enable LP.Int	Enable Raster Int	Raster Comp.8

Address		Bit 7	Bit 6	Bit 5	Bit 4	Bit 3	Bit 2	Bit 1	Bit 0
$FF0B	11	Raster Comp.7	Raster Comp.6	Raster Comp.5	Raster Comp.4	Raster Comp.3	Raster Comp.2	Raster Comp.1	Raster Comp.0
$FF0C	12	N/C	N/C	N/C	N/C	N/C	N/C	Cursor Bit 9	Cursor Bit 8
$FF0D	13	Cursor Bit 7	Cursor Bit 6	Cursor Bit 5	Cursor Bit 4	Cursor Bit 3	Cursor Bit 2	Cursor Bit 1	Cursor Bit 0
$FF0E	14	Voice 1 Bit 7	Voice 1 Bit 6	Voice 1 Bit 5	Voice 1 Bit 4	Voice 1 Bit 3	Voice 1 Bit 2	Voice 1 Bit 1	Voice 1 Bit 0
$FF0F	15	Voice 2 Bit 7	Voice 2 Bit 6	Voice 2 Bit 5	Voice 2 Bit 4	Voice 2 Bit 3	Voice 2 Bit 2	Voice 2 Bit 1	Voice 2 Bit 0
$FF10	16	N/C	N/C	N/C	N/C	N/C	N/C	Voice 2 Bit 9	Voice 2 Bit 8
$FF11	17	Sound Reload	Noise	Voice 2 Select	Voice 1 Select	Volume Bit 3	Volume Bit 2	Volume Bit 1	Volume Bit 0
$FF12	18	N/C	N/C	Bit map base 2	Bit map base 1	Bit map base 0	ROM/RAM Select	Voice 1 Bit 9	Voice 1 Bit 8
$FF13	19	Char. base 5	Char. base 4	Char. base 3	Char. base 2	Char. base 1	Char. base 0	Single Clock	Status
$FF14	20	Video Matrix4	Video Matrix3	Video Matrix2	Video Matrix1	Video Matrix0	N/C	N/C	N/C
$FF15	21	N/C	Bkgrnd Lum 2	Bkgrnd Lum 1	Bkgrnd Lum 0	Bkgrnd Col 3	Bkgrnd Col 2	Bkgrnd Col 1	Bkgrnd Col 0
$FF16	22	N/C	Charctr Lum 2	Charctr Lum 1	Charctr Lum 0	Charctr Col 3	Charctr Col 2	Charctr Col 1	Charctr Col 0

Address		Bit 7	Bit 6	Bit 5	Bit 4	Bit 3	Bit 2	Bit 1	Bit 0
$FF17	23	N/C	Multi 1 Lum 2	Multi 1 Lum 1	Multi 1 Lum 0	Multi 1 Col 3	Multi 1 Col 2	Multi 1 Col 1	Multi 1 Col 0
$FF18	24	N/C	Multi 2 Lum 2	Multi 2 Lum 1	Multi 2 Lum 0	Multi 2 Col 3	Multi 2 Col 2	Multi 2 Col 1	Multi 2 Col 0
$FF19	25	N/C	Border Lum 2	Border Lum 1	Border Lum 0	Border Col 3	Border Col 2	Border Col 1	Border Col 0
$FF1A	26	N/C	N/C	N/C	N/C	N/C	N/C	Bit map Reload9	Bit map Reload8
$FF1B	27	Bit map Reload7	Bit map Reload6	Bit map Reload5	Bit map Reload4	Bit map Reload3	Bit map Reload2	Bit map Reload1	Bit map Reload0
$FF1C	28	N/C	N/C	N/C	N/C	N/C	N/C	N/C	Vert. Line 8
$FF1D	29	Vert. Line 7	Vert. Line 6	Vert. Line 5	Vert. Line 4	Vert. Line 3	Vert. Line 2	Vert. Line 1	Vert. Line 0
$FF1E	30	Horiz Pos 8	Horiz Pos 7	Horiz Pos 6	Horiz Pos 5	Horiz Pos 4	Horiz Pos 3	Horiz Pos 2	Horiz Pos 1
$FF1F	31	N/C	Blink Bit 3	Blink Bit 2	Blink Bit 1	Blink Bit 0	Vert. Sub 2	Vert. Sub 1	Vert. Sub 0
$FF3E	62	R.O.M. SELECT							
$FF3F	63	R.A.M. SELECT							

THE TED CHIP REGISTER DESCRIPTION

Registers #0 to #5: Internal Timers

The TED chip has three 16-bit interval timers on board. Each timer is physically divided into two 8-bit registers, occupying two successive memory locations. The timers decrement at a fixed frequency, 884 KHz for PAL systems and 894 KHz for NTSC systems, and will generate an interrupt upon decrementing to zero.

The timers should be initialised using the following procedure:

- (a) Disable all Interrupts
- (b) Write low byte of Timer
- (c) Write high byte of Timer
- (d) Enable desired Interrupts.

Note: It is essential that there be no more than 125 microseconds delay between writing the low byte and then the high byte, otherwise timing count errors will occur.

Timer #1 is a sequence interval timer comprising register 0, low byte, and register 1, high byte. Register 0 and 1, when written to, initiate the reload value of the timer. When Timer #1 decrements to zero, an interrupt is issued, then the Timer is reset to the reload value and the cycle begins again.

Timers #2 & #3 are free running counters. Upon decrementing to the zero, the timers roll over to $FFFF and continue counting. Writing to timer 2 or 3 registers will load directly into the active count. Reading these registers yields the current count.

Register #6: Screen Format

Bits 0-2 of this register determine the vertical scroll position. Bit 3 is the 24/25 row select bit. Setting bit 3 high will yield 25 rows, while clearing this bit will yield 24 rows. To perform a vertical scroll, bit 3 should be cleared, and bits 0-2 should be either incremented or decremented, depending on whether a downwards or upwards scroll is desired. If vertical scrolling is not required, then bits 0-2 should set to equal 3, and bit 3 should be set.

Bit 4 is the screen blanking bit. If set high, then the normal screen is displayed. If cleared, then the screen is blanked and all TED fetches are disabled, permitting the processor to run at almost twice the speed (1.788MHz for NTSC and 1.768MHz for PAL).

Bit 5 enables bit map mode when set high.

Bit 6 enables extended colour mode when set high.

Bit 7 is used for chip testing and must remain cleared.

Register #7: Screen Format

Bits 0-2 of this register determine the horizontal scroll position. Bit 3 is the 39/40 column select bit, that when set high provides for 40 character columns. In this case, bits 0-2 should be set to equal zero. When bit 3 is cleared, 38 column mode is selected, allowing horizontal scrolling to occur. If Bits 0-2 are incremented, then the screen scrolls to the right. If they are decremented, then the screen will scroll to the left.

Bit 4 enables the multicolour mode when set high.

Bit 5 is 'freeze' bit which, when set high, inhibits TED from incrementing the horizontal and vertical position, and the timers.

Bit 6 selects either the PAL video standard when cleared, or the NTSC standard when cleared when set.

Bit 7 is the reverse video off bit. Normally bit 7 is cleared, and there are 128 character patterns available. Characters can be reversed by setting the MSB of the video matrix pointer high, i.e. add 128 to the screen code values. This enables TED to invert character data, and hence display reversed characters. If an alternate character set of 256 characters is required, then Bit 7 can be set high, disabling the reverse video feature and allowing the MSB of the video matrix to define the additional characters.

Register #8: Keyboard Latch

This register is the keyboard latch. Writing to this register causes the keyboard matrix to be scanned and latches the appropriate data. When this register is read, data that had been previously latched can be obtained.

Register #9: Interrupt Status

Register 9 is the interrupt source register. Any TED interrupts are recorded by the appropriate bit being cleared. Possible interrupt sources are:

    Bit 1 — Raster Interrupt
    Bit 2 — Light Pen (for later expansion)
    Bit 3 — Timer 1 Interrupt
    Bit 4 — Timer 2 Interrupt
    Bit 6 — Timer 3 Interrupt
    Bit 7 — Interrupt Request

Individual interrupt bits can be reset by setting them high.

Register 1∅: Interrupt Mask

This register is the mask for the Interrupt status register. Setting a bit high in the Interrupt Mask Register enables the corresponding bit in the Interrupt Register to flag a future interrupt.

Bit ∅ is the MSB of the Raster Compare Register and is not part of the mask (see register 11 for description).

Register #11: Raster Compare

In an NTSC television system, 262 raster lines are generated (∅ to 261), while for a PAL system, 312 lines (∅ to 311) per screen. To account for all raster lines, a 9 bit register is required. Register 11 contains the low order 8 bits, while the 9th bit is the least significant bit of the Interrupt Mask Register (bit ∅ of register 1∅). The Raster Compare Register is an interrupt source. When the Raster Line count equals the value of the Raster Compare Register, an interrupt is generated. This technique can be used to perform split screen operations. Since there may be an appreciable delay in processing this interrupt, it is generated 8 cycles before the character window, thus minimising screen flicker. For a 25 row display, visible raster lines are from 4 to 2∅3.

Register #12: Cursor Position (MSB)

This register contains the two most significant bits of the cursor position register. Bit 1 of this register contains bit 9 and bit ∅ contains bit 8 of the cursor position.

Register #13: Cursor Position (LSB)

The 8 low order bits of the cursor position are contained in register 13. The Cursor Position Register comprises 1∅ bits, giving 1∅24 distinct cursor locations.

Register #14: Voice #1 Frequency (LSBs)

This register contains the low byte of the frequency base for voice 1. This voice can have only a square wave oscillator as its source.

Register #15: Voice #2 Frequency (LSBs)

This register contains the low order 8 bits of the frequency base for voice 2. This voice may have either a white noise or a square wave oscillator, selectable by a bit in register #17.

Register #16: Voice 2 Frequency (MSBs)

The two MSBs of the voice 2 frequency register are contained in bits 1 & 0 of this register.

Register #17: Sound Control

Bits 0-3 of this register are assigned as master volume control, 0 being off to 8 or greater being the loudest volume setting.

Bit 4 enables voice 1 when set high.

Bit 5 enables voice 2 with a square oscillator when set high.

Bit 6 enables voice 2 with a white noise oscillator when set high.

Note: Bit 5, if set, will override bit 6 thus producing a square wave output.

Bit 7 is a test bit.

Register #18: Bit Map Base

Another multi function register, Bits 0 and 1 are the MSBs of voice 2 frequency register.

Bit 2 is used to indicate where the TED chip will fetch its character and dot data from. If set high, ROM is selected, otherwise, if cleared, then RAM is chosen.

Bits 3-5 are used to determine where the bit map base resides. During TED dot fetches, the 3 MSBs of the address lines, A15-A13, are written into bits 5 to bit 3.

Register #19: Character Base

Bit 0 of this register is a read only status bit describing the state of the two phantom registers 62 and 63. If it is high, then TED is operating from ROM memory. If it is cleared, then TED registers are not accessible.

Bit 1 when set high forces single clock mode, inhibiting double clock speed during horizontal blanking.

Bits 2 to 7 comprise the character data base. The six bits give 64 separate areas for character data, in 1K increments. To change character sets, the character base register should be set to the appropriate value, depending on where the new character resides, and then the ROM/RAM bank select bit (bit 2 of register #18) should be cleared. TED will now refer to that part of RAM for its character information.

Register #2Ø: Video Matrix Base

The top five bits of this register are what make up the Video Matrix Base Register. This register determines which 2K block of memory will serve as the Video Matrix pointers and Attribute data (screen and colour memory). By careful use of the Raster Compare Register, a split screen could be set up having two different sets of screen and colour data coming from different areas of memory.

Register #21: Background Colour

This register comprises a 4 bit colour code and a 3 bit luminence code. This yields eight separate luminences for all 16 colours.

Bits Ø-3 define the background colour.

Bits 4-6 determine the luminence of the background colour.

Register #22: Character Colour

Bits Ø-3 define the character colour.

Bits 4-6 define the luminence of the character colour.

Register #23: Multicolour 1

Bits Ø-3 define the colour of multicolour 1, useable only in extended colour mode.

Bits 4-6 define the luminence for this colour.

Register #24: Multicolour 2

Bits Ø-3 define the colour of multicolour 2, also only available in extended colour mode.

Bits 4-6 define the luminence information for this colour.

Note: Whenever this register is changed, all pixels in multicolour 2 also change to the new colour.

Register #25: Border Colour

Bits Ø-3 define the border colour.

Bits 4-6 define the luminence.

Register #26: Character Position Reload (MSBs)

Bits 1 and 0 comprise the MSB of the Character Position Reload Register. This register is used by TED to count the row on which it will display characters. Each time a row, comprising 8 raster lines, has been displayed on the screen, the register will be incremented by 40.

Register #27: Character Position Reload (LSBs)

This register comprises the low order 8 bits of the Character Position Reload register.

Register #28: Vertical Raster Count (MSBs)

Bit 0 is the MSB of the 9 bit Vertical Line Register. This register is used by the TED chip to count the current raster line being displayed, and ranges from 0 to 261 for the NTSC standard, or 0 to 311 for the PAL standard.

Register #29: Vertical Raster Count (LSBs)

The low order 8 bits of the Vertical Raster Count Register.

Register #30: Horizontal Position

This register comprises the upper 8 bits of the 9 bit Horizontal Position Register. The LSB of the register is not available as it changes too fast to be of any use. This register increments from 0 to 455 but because only the top 8 bits are available, the actual value of the register ranges from 0 to 288. Since this register clocks over at a fast rate, it could be successfully used to generate random numbers.

Register #31: Blink

Bits 0-3 comprise the Blink rate register which contains the current count of the Blink Rate Timer. This register is incremented once per screen.

When this register overflows, a 2Hz signal is generated to initialise the cursor reverse video and any flashing characters.

Bits 4-6 comprise the Vertical Subaddress register which counts the eight raster lines per character row.

Registers 62 and 63

These registers aren't really on the TED chip but instead are used to control the TED system memory map. A write to register 62 causes ROM to be selected in the $8000 to $FFFF range, excluding memory mapped I/O and TED from $FD00 to $FF3F. When register 63 is written to, RAM is instead selected over that range, thus BASIC may be switched out.

Note: All TED registers are read/write, so care should be taken when writing to registers 26 through to 31, as they are internal control registers. Writing to them can result in the screen flickering.

Appendix 7

The Makings Of A Good Assembler

The time will come when you will probably decide on the switch to using a full assembler, with features far superior to those found in Tedmon. You will quickly learn that using Tedmon to assemble programs of medium to large size is, to say the least, very tedious and messy. For example, you may have relative instructions that branch forward several locations:

```
2000          BEQ $2008
```

To obtain the address of this branch, you would have had to count the number of instructions between the original instruction and its destination, adding this to the original address. This example is only one illustration of the limitation of using a simple assembler.

Take the following program, which displays the characters from 'A' to 'Z' (screen codes 1 to 26) on the top line of the screen:

```
2000 LDA    #$01
2002 STA    $03
2004 LDY    #$00
2006 LDA    $03
2008 STA    $0C00,Y
200B INC    $03
200D INY
200E CPY    #$1A
2010 BNE    $2006
2012 BRK
```

While this program is extremely short, it is still fairly difficult to follow without some form of commentary. The same program written with a full assembler might look something like:

```
10          ORG  $2000     ; START PROGRAM AT $2000
15 SCREEN =      $0C00     ; DEFINE BASE ADDRESS FOR SCREEN
20 CHAR   =      $03       ; DEFINE CHARACTER STORAGE LOCATION
25 ;
30 ; Y REGISTER USED AS AN INDEX TO THE SCREEN,
```

```
35  ; AND AS THE COUNTER TO 26 (26 CHARS)
40  ;
45            LDA   #$01      ; LOAD THE VALUE FOR CHARACTER 'A'
50            STA   CHAR      ; STORE THIS IN 'CHAR' LOCATION
55            LDY   #$00      ; INITiALISE OUR COUNTER
60  REPEAT LDA   CHAR      ; LOAD THE CURRENT CHARACTER VALUE
65            STA   SCREEN,Y  ; STORE THIS TO THE SCREEN
70            INC   CHAR      ; UPDATE CHARACTER VALUE
75            INY             ; UPDATE COUNTER AND SCREEN POS.
80            CPY   #$1A      ; HAVE 26 CHARS BEEN DISPLAYED?
85            BNE   REPEAT    ; NO, SO GO BACK, DISPLAY NEXT
90            BRK             ; EXIT FROM PROGRAM
```

As you will have noticed, a full assembler is oriented towards making life easier for the programmer, not the computer. The example given above may have seemed a trifle 'over-documented', but it illustrates the kind of documentation that can be implemented in programs.

With a full assembler, labels may be used in place of absolute addresses, so that the programmer does not have to perform any calculations for relative addresses or offsets, as is the case for Tedmon. Line numbers, or some other method of organization, is used primarily for editing and debugging purposes.

The strange looking 'ORG' statement found on line 10 is known as a 'pseudo-op' or 'assembler directive'. Assemblers need additional information about such things as 'where' to assemble the source code, or whether to print it out. Line 10 of the above program is simply letting the assembler know that it should start the assembly with the first instruction at location $2000.

With most assemblers, you can store your source code (i.e. unassembled code) onto tape or disk; you can print it out, and you can insert and delete lines at will. Below is a list of some of the features that you should consider. When deciding on an assembler for your own use, you may decide that all, or only some, of these features are needed.

Labels

Almost all assemblers support both the use of standard labels and of standard addresses, for use as parameters in instructions. This feature should be high on your priority list, as it alleviates the need to calculate resulting addresses, thus greatly decreasing your code generation times.

There are basically two types of labels that are incurred when working with assembly language:

INTERNAL LABELS: These are references to locations within the program that is being assembled. For example:

```
5         ORG  $2000
10        JMP  OUT
  .
  .
  .
30 OUT  RTS
```

In this case the label 'OUT' is called an internal label, because the location 'OUT' resides within the program.

EXTERNAL LABELS: These are references to locations outside the program that is being assembled. For example:

```
5         ORG  $2000
10 SET  =    $FFD2
  .
  .
  .
30        JSR  SET
```

In this case the label 'SET' is called an external label, because it is a reference to a location outside the program.

Error Returns

Here is another area that should not be overlooked. There is nothing more infuriating than an assembler that returns with 'ERROR', without an explanation as to what has actually happened. Fortunately, these assemblers seem to have become extinct, and you should find that nearly all of the assemblers on the market will display a full error message, or at least an error number, with a corresponding message section in the assembler's manual. You should bear this in mind when purchasing an assembler, remembering that debugging usually takes up a fair amount of time in the development of any program.

Assembler Directives

This section illustrates a series of instructions that may or may not be important in the assembly of your programs. Assembler directives are additional commands to aid in formatting your listings, reserve and manipulate memory, and generally keep the assembler running smoothly. Though the names for these commands might vary from assembler to assembler, a description of a few are given below.

• Assembly Start Location: All assemblers will have some method of allocating a start address for assembly of the source code. It can be taken for granted that this feature will be implemented, in one form or another, in whatever assembler that you buy.

• Reserve Memory: This command is used to reserve memory that can be used by your program. It enables you to create blank areas for storing data such as a list of names and addresses. You should find that most assemblers will support this feature in one form or another.

• Allocate Values to Memory: This is used to store constant values in memory. An example might be the storage of the text that makes up a title screen for one of your programs. This feature should incorporate the following:

— the ability to store values in the form of numbers.
— the ability to store strings (e.g. "hello") in ASCII format.

• Format A Printout: This command will generally display an assembly printout in a tabulated form. A graphic example paints the picture as to how this command can make life easier:

UNFORMATTED	FORMATTED

```
UNFORMATTED              FORMATTED

LDA    #$01              LDA #$01
LOOP   STA $03    LOOP   STA $03
INX                      INX
BNE    LOOP              BNE LOOP
;REPEAT TASK                       ;REPEAT TASK
INY                      INY
BNE    LOOP              BNE LOOP
  .                        .
  .                        .
  .                        .
```

By aligning the fields into Label, Mnemonic, Operand/s, Comments order, the listing becomes a lot easier to read. This feature is not entirely necessary but is very handy in producing 'pretty printouts'.

• Number Systems: A good assembler will accept numbers in the following bases:

Decimal	:— base ten
Hexadecimal	:— base sixteen
Binary	:— base two
Octal	:— base eight

However, with the use of octal now declining, an assembler supporting the former bases will definitely suffice. You will find that Decimal is handy as a human interface (we use this base in everyday life), and that hexadecimal is useful when dealing with addresses.

Binary is useful when dealing with individual bits (as in masking). As a general rule, the assembler should use the following nomenclature:

Decimals have no prefix (e.g. 10,34)
Hexadecimals have a dollar sign as a prefix (e.g. $12,$8065)
Binary numbers have a percentage sign as a prefix (e.g. %100 11101,%1110)
Octals have the 'commercial at' sign as a prefix (e.g. @76,@34)

Creating Large Programs

When using an assembler, the source code is usually much larger than the object code that is generated. For example:

```
LDA #$08
STA $200A
```

generates five bytes of object code, whereas the source code is probably stored as twenty to thirty bytes. The C-16 has 16 kilobytes of useable memory, so that approximately 16 kilobytes of object code could be stored in memory. To generate this amount of object code would require between sixty and a hundred kilobytes of source code, depending on the method that the assembler uses to store this code. The C-16 could not possibly cope with this volume of source code at one time. The method used to solve this problem is to link one source file to another, with each file being assembled separately, the result being one large program. If you are only planning on writing small programs then this feature may be unnecessary.

At this point it may be worth mentioning that there are several ways that an assembler can generate the resultant object code for your program:

- It could store the object code directly into memory. This technique could pose a serious problem, due to the fact that with the C-16's memory limitations you would only have enough room for fairly small programs. You must not forget that an assembler with many of the features that we are now discussing would probably need at least 10 kilobytes of memory to operate.

- Another method that an assembler can use is to store the object code onto tape or disk. Using this method, the full 16 kilobytes can be used, with no conflict between the program and the assembler.

There are other variations on these two themes, each with its advantages and disadvantages. The method used to store object code should be treated as a crucial point when buying an assembler for any machine with memory limitations.

Macros

More and more assemblers are beginning to support a feature called 'macros'. A macro is a predefined series of instructions, which are named using a label. After a macro has been defined, subsequent references to its 'name' will insert the associated code from its definition. Parameters can also be sent to a macro. An example might be:

```
10  MACRO INCBYTE INC  ?1
15                 BNE  ?3
20                 INC  ?2
25  ?3             NOP
30  MACRO-END.
```

At this stage, the macro has been defined. Now, if line 50 had:

```
50                 INCBYTE $05,$06
```

then the following code would be inserted:

```
                   INC  $05
                   BNE  L01
                   INC  $06
          L01      NOP
```

which corresponds to the code, as defined in the macro, with the parameters (?1,?2,?3) being filled in.

Macros are extremely handy when a piece of code is used over and over again, but with different parameters.

Mathematical Functions

Most assemblers will support the use of simple mathematical functions, typically addition, subtraction, multiplication and division. These functions aid in alleviating the programmer from calculations. A simple example might be:

```
10  BASE   = $03
15  BASE2  = $04
20  BASE3  = $06
25         INC  BASE
30         INC  BASE
35         INC  BASE3
```

Now with an assembler utilising mathematical functions, this could have been entered as:

```
10  BASE   = $03
15         INC  BASE
20         INC  BASE+1
25         INC  BASE*2
```

This feature should not really be treated as an absolute necessity, but merely as a very handy 'extra'.

The Library Option

Some assemblers allow you to store sections of source codes onto tape or disk, which can be called in and used as a part of any other program. If, say, you had written a routine that could handle input from a joystick, then you could store this routine as a library routine, and use it in any other program that requires a joystick routine such as this one.

Text Handling Functions

Assemblers are now starting to incorporate features that have traditionally belonged to word processors. With some assemblers, you are now able to move blocks of source code from one place to another, search and replace within the source code, as well as a host of other functions which make programming much easier. This is another feature that can be considered as an 'extra', although assemblers implementing it will enable faster generation of source code, through ease of use in editing.

Offset option

This option allows you to assemble the source code, as if you were to locate it at one address, but the assembler will store it at another address. This makes it possible to load code at one address, and then have it transferred to its proper operating address when it is required. It also aids in the programming of programmable chips, known as EPROMS (erasable, programmable ROM chips).

In this section, we have covered a few of the most common 'features' that may be incorporated into an assembler. If you take some time to examine a few assemblers on the market, you will find that there are a number of features that have not been covered in this section. I have outlined what I consider to be the most important areas of an assembler's design. It should now be left to individual preference as to what assembler you purchase.

Appendix 8

ASCII and CHR$ Codes

This table shows you what characters will appear if you PRINT CHR$(X), for all possible values of X. It will also show the values obtained by typing PRINT ASC("X"), where X is any character you can type. This is useful in evaluating the character received in a GET statement, converting upper/lower case, and printing character based commands (like switch to upper/lower case) that could not be enclosed in quotes.

1) CHR$ Value Codes

Character	CHR$ Code	Character	CHR$ Code
	0		
	1		21
	2		22
STOP	3		23
	4		24
WHITE	5		25
	6		26
	7		27
DISABLES SHIFT KEY	8	RED	28
ENABLES SHIFT KEY	9	CSRS →	29
	10	GREEN	30
	11	BLUE	31
	12	space	32
RETURN	13	!	33
Lower case switch	14	"	34
	15	#	35
	16	$	36
CRSR ↓	17	%	37
RVS ON	18	&	38
CLR/HOME	19	'	39
INST/DEL	20	(	40

135

Character	CHR$ Code	Character	CHR$ Code
)	41	P	80
*	42	Q	81
+	43	R	82
,	44	S	83
–	45	T	84
.	46	U	85
/	47	V	86
0	48	W	87
1	49	X	88
2	50	Y	89
3	51	Z	90
4	52	[	91
5	53	£	92
6	54	]	93
7	55	↑	94
8	56	←	95
9	57	▤	96
:	58	♠	97
;	59	▯	98
<	60	▤	99
=	61	▤	100
>	62	▢	101
?	63	▤	102
@	64	▯	103
A	65	▯	104
B	66	◪	105
C	67	◪	106
D	68	◪	107
E	69	▢	108
F	70	◪	109
G	71	◪	110
H	72	▢	111
I	73	▢	112
J	74	■	113
K	75	▤	114
L	76	♥	115
M	77	▯	116
N	78	◪	117
O	79	⊠	118

Character	CHR$ Code	Character	CHR$ Code
▢	119	PURPLE	156
♣	120	CRSR ←	157
▯	121	YELLOW	158
◆	122	CYAN	159
▦	123	space	160
▯	124	▮	161
▯	125	▬	162
π	126	▭	163
◣	127	▯	164
	128	▯	165
	129	▓	166
FLASH ON	130	▯	167
SHIFT RUN/STOP.	131	▬	168
FLASH OFF	132	◪	169
f1	133	▯	170
f3	134	▯	171
f5	135	▯	172
f7	136	▯	173
f2	137	▯	174
f4	138	▬	175
f6	139	▯	176
f8	140	▦	177
SHIFT RETURN	141	▦	178
Upper case switch	142	▯	179
	143	▯	180
BLACK	144	▯	181
CRSR ↑	145	▯	182
RVS OFF	146	▭	183
CLR/HOME	147	▭	184
INST/DEL	148	▬	185
◲	149	▯	186
⊠	150	▯	187
◯	151	▯	188
♣	152	▯	189
▢	153	▯	190
◆	154	▮	191
▦	155		

Codes 192-223 are the same as 96-127
Codes 224-254 are the same as 160-190
Code 255 is the same as code 126

Appendix 9

Screen Display Codes

The screen codes listed below correspond to the values that should be stored in the appropriate location in screen memory to display the desired character.

Two sets are available, but not at the same time. To select the other set, the Commodore logo key should be depressed, followed by the shift key.

Character Set 1	Character Set 2	Screen Code
@		0
A	a	1
B	b	2
C	c	3
D	d	4
E	e	5
F	f	6
G	g	7
H	h	8
I	i	9
J	j	10
K	k	11
L	l	12
M	m	13
N	n	14
O	o	15
P	p	16
Q	q	17
R	r	18
S	s	19
T	t	20
U	u	21
V	v	22

Character Set 1	Character Set 2	Screen Code
W	w	23
X	x	24
Y	y	25
Z	z	26
[		27
£		28
]		29
↑		30
←		31
space		32
!		33
"		34
#		35
$		36
%		37
&		38
'		39
(		40
)		41
*		42
+		43
,		44
−		45
.		46
/		47
0		48
1		49
2		50
3		51
4		52
5		53
6		54
7		55
8		56
9		57
÷		58
;		59
<		60

Character Set 1	Character Set 2	Screen Code
=		61
>		62
?		63
		64
	A	65
	B	66
	C	67
	D	68
	E	69
	F	70
	G	71
	H	72
	I	73
	J	74
	K	75
	L	76
	M	77
	N	78
	O	79
	P	80
	Q	81
	R	82
	S	83
	T	84
	U	85
	V	86
	W	87
	X	88
	Y	89
	Z	90
		91
		92
		93
		94
		95
space		96
		97
		98

Character	Character	Screen
Set 1	Set 2	Code
⬚		99
⬚		100
⬚		101
■		102
⬚		103
⬛		104
◪	%	105
⬚		106
⬚		107
⬚		108
⬚		109
⬚		110
⬚		111
⬚		112
⬚		113
⬚		114
⬚		115
⬚		116
⬚		117
⬚		118
⬚		119
⬚		120
⬚		121
⬚		122
⬚		123
⬚		124
⬚		125
⬚		126
◪		127

Codes 128-255 produce reversed images of codes 0-127

GLOSSARY

ASSEMBLER

This is a program which takes a program written in ASSEMBLY LANGUAGE, a form which the programmer can understand but which is meaningless to the microprocessor, and converts it to MACHINE CODE which the microprocessor can understand but which is difficult for the programmer to work with.

ASSEMBLY CODE

See ASSEMBLY LANGUAGE

ASSEMBLY LANGUAGE

This is a program written out in a form the programmer can understand but which means nothing directly to the MICROPROCESSOR until run through an ASSEMBLER. Any large MACHINE CODE program will be written via ASSEMBLY LANGUAGE (see ASSEMBLER).

BINARY

Base 2. Used by almost all computers. Each digit can have only two possible values — 0 and 1 (electrically on and off etc.). By making the possible value of the digit worth more depending on its position as we do in decimal etc.

$$145$$
$$= 1 \times 100 + 4 \times 10 + 5 \times 1$$

binary becomes etc.

$$1011$$
$$= 1 \times 8 + 0 \times 4 + 1 \times 2 + 1 \times 1 = 11 \text{ decimal}$$

BIT

One BINARY digit, which can only take the value of a one or a zero. When strung together it can be used to form a larger number (see BINARY, see BYTE).

BUFFER

An area of memory set aside for temporary storage of data. Usually used in relation to input/output functions.

BYTE

The basic unit of the computer's MEMORY. One MEMORY LOCATION can hold 1 BYTE of information. Each BYTE is made up of 8 BITS and can store a number between 0 and 255. This number may represent a character, a numeric value, or part of a microprocessor instruction. Can be strung together like BITS to form larger numbers (see BINARY).

CHARACTER

Generally any symbol which can be put on the screen by pressing a key on the keyboard. Any symbol (alphanumeric) you can write (that is not a drawing or a picture) is a CHARACTER. NOTE: for an exception see GRAPHICS CHARACTERS.

CHARACTER SET

The set of all CHARACTERS which can be printed on the TEXT screen.

DECIMAL

Base 10. Our normal everyday way of counting is called the decimal number system.

DISASSEMBLER

A program which takes a MACHINE CODE program and prints it out in ASSEMBLY LANGUAGE so the programmer can read it (see ASSEMBLER).

DUMP

A memory DUMP is a display of the contents of memory in a numerical or character form (not as ASSEMBLY CODE instructions).

GRAPHICS

In GRAPHICS mode you can display anything on the screen that you can display using the resolution of the dots the computer puts out (the size of a full stop).

GRAPHICS CHARACTER

Part of the CHARACTER SET is made up of CHARACTERS which are only shapes and hold no symbolic meaning. These are GRAPHICS CHARACTERS.

HEXADECIMAL

Base 16 (sometimes called HEX). Base 16 is used in dealing with machine code because it is an easy way of dealing with BINARY numbers, which very soon become cumbersome. A BYTE is divided into two sections of four binary BITS, each capable of storing a number from

$0 \rightarrow 15$. The number is represented by a HEX digit $0 \rightarrow 9$, $A \rightarrow F$. Thus a byte can be displayed by using two HEX digits. A **$** sign is usually used to signify a HEX number.

INTERRUPT

An interrupt is an electronic signal sent to the microprocessor, by a peripheral or a chip within the computer, to notify it of something happening in the outside world.

MACHINE CODE

Sometimes called MACHINE LANGUAGE, it is the way of describing a program that can be directly run by the MICROPROCESSOR. A MACHINE CODE program is made up of a string of numbers which may be put into the computer by the programmer in HEX, or assembled using an ASSEMBLER from a program written in ASSEMBLY CODE.

MACHINE LANGUAGE

See MACHINE CODE.

MEMORY

Boxes at pigeonholes within the computer which are used to hold numbers, machine language instructions and characters. Each box can hold only 1 BYTE of memory at a time. The C64 has 64K (65536) bytes of memory.

MEMORY ADDRESS

Each memory box has a number from 0 to 65535 which is used to refer to it from among the 65536 within the computer. A number used for this purpose is called an address.

MEMORY LOCATION

An easier way of saying memory at address.

MICROPROCESSOR

The central processing and control unit of the computer. It can be compared to the human brain (as long as you realise that the brain is of comparatively immense power with huge memory and enormously complex programs). The microprocessor controls all movement of data, all decisions and all calculations within the computer.

TEXT

In TEXT mode you can only display CHARACTERS which are in the CHARACTER SET on the screen (see GRAPHICS).

VECTOR

Is the name given to bytes in RAM which store the address of a ROM routine. These bytes are used so that the process of the operating system or basic calling ROM input/output routines may be accessed by the user. The progammer will set these RAM bytes to point to his own program to handle input/output in his own way.

ZERO PAGE

Another name for the first 256 bytes of memory from $0 to $255.

You may also enjoy...

C16

commodore 16
GAMES BOOK

CAMERON DUFFY   RICHARD WOOLCOCK

You may also enjoy...

Mastering the Commodore 64

Mark Greenshields